SCARVES
AND COWLS

SCARVES
AND COWLS

36 QUICK AND STYLISH KNITS

FIONA GOBLE

CICO BOOKS
LONDON NEW YORK

Published in 2014 by CICO Books
An imprint of Ryland Peters & Small
20–21 Jockey's Fields, London WC1R 4BW
519 Broadway, 5th Floor, New York NY 10012

www.rylandpeters.com

10 9 8 7 6 5 4 3 2 1

A CIP catalog record for this book is
available from the Library of Congress
and the British Library.

ISBN: 978-1-78249-139-2

Printed in China

Editor: Kate Haxell
Designer: Vicky Rankin
Photographer: Terry Benson
Stylist and Photographic Art Direction: Luis Peral
Hair and Make-up: Rose Angus

For digital editions, visit
www.cicobooks.com/apps.php

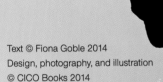

Contents

Introduction

A selection of contemporary neckwear is essential for every fashionista's wardrobe. And with this book, you won't have to spend weeks on end creating your bespoke collection, because there are plenty of straightforward designs for both new and intermediate knitters.

Scarves and their close relatives are such a brilliantly simple way of keeping those cool breezes from whistling round your neck and making you hunch your shoulders. But they're also a great way to add a dose of color, texture, and pizzazz to your favorite outfits.

This collection of more than 30 scarves and cowls for adults and children includes styles to suit every taste, different knitting skills—and pretty much every budget. If you want your scarf to accessorize your country attire for a winter stroll on the beach, there's a fantastic selection to choose from. But if you want to knit something lighter to keep the chill at bay on a cool summer evening, then we've got the solution for that, too.

But it's not all about knitting something that suits your style: if you're busy doing lots of other things as well as knitting, then you need a project that will fit in with your busy lifestyle. That's

why I've included several projects that you can whip up in just an evening or two.

If money and time are a little tight, there are even some projects you can knit from a single ball of yarn. But if you've got a bit more time and your budget is a little more elastic, your choice will obviously be that bit wider.

If you're brand-new to knitting, or haven't picked up your needles for a while, the book includes projects where all you'll need to know is how to cast on, knit a basic stitch, and bind (cast) off. But if you've mastered the purl stitch, too, there'll be several more projects that you can add to your list of possibles.

And if you've already got a bit of knitting practice under your belt and you're ready for a challenge, the book also includes some beautiful lacy and cabled scarves. These are the perfect choice for those who want to dip their toes into the world of less-than-basic knitting patterns—without committing too much time and money.

I've loved creating all the styles in this book—and I hope you'll love creating your own versions and adding your own twist to the designs.

Knits

From super-simple scarves that are perfect for novice knitters, to textured knits that include easy lace and chunky cables, these pages are packed with fab projects for you to knit.

Pompom scarf
instructions on page 72

"Beware making pompoms is addictive!"

Twist headband
instructions on page 73

"Hello duckie.
How are you today?"

Long striped scarf
instructions on page 74

Lacy knit neck warmer
instructions on page 76

Roll-neck capelet
instructions on page 78

Pull-through scarf with flower
instructions on page 80

Patchwork scarf
instructions on page 77

Tweedy keyhole scarf
instructions on page 82

"Tweedy is as tweedy does, and this tweedy's easy."

Boa scarf
instructions on page 84

Lace ripple scarf
instructions on page 85

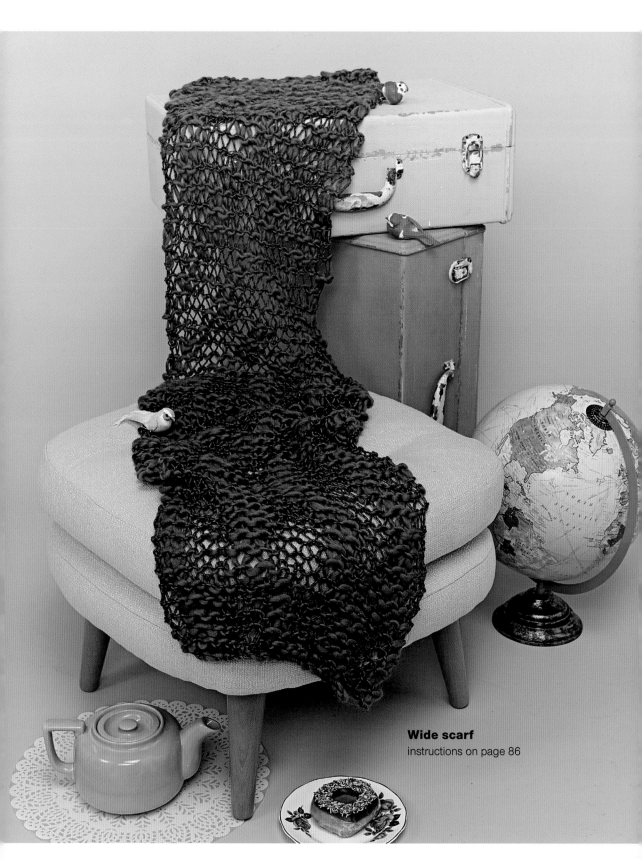

Wide scarf
instructions on page 86

Rib scarf
instructions on page 87

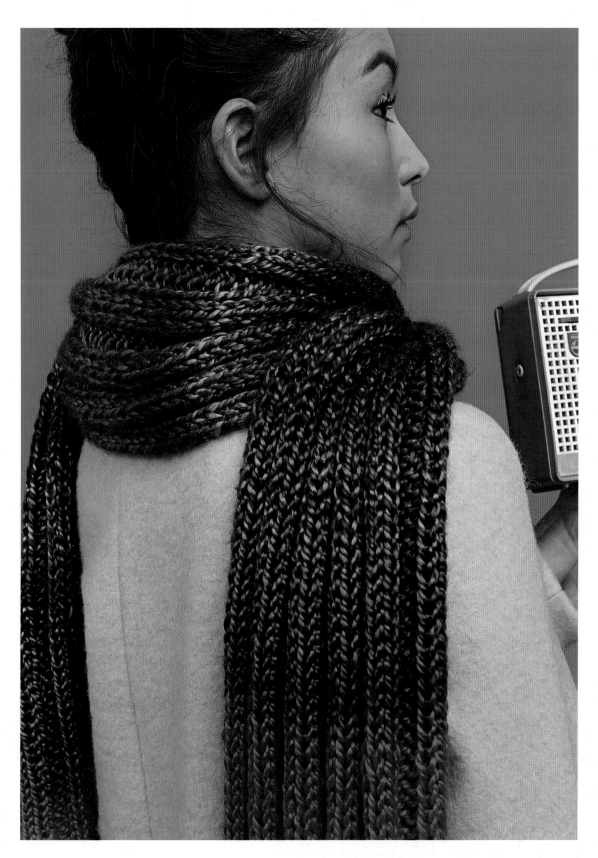

Waffle-knit neck warmer
instructions on page 88

Mega-chunky cowl
instructions on page 89

Fur collar
instructions on page 90

"Furry and super-cute: what's not to like?"

Chunky ribbed cowl
instructions on page 91

Long scarf with pockets
instructions on page 92

Lacy ruffled scarf
instructions on page 93

Skinny lace scarf
instructions on page 94

**Chunky cable
neck warmer**
instructions on page 95

Simple capelet
instructions on page 96

*"All you need is tea
and warm socks."*

Fine lace-knit capelet
instructions on page 97

47

Bandana with tassels
instructions on page 98

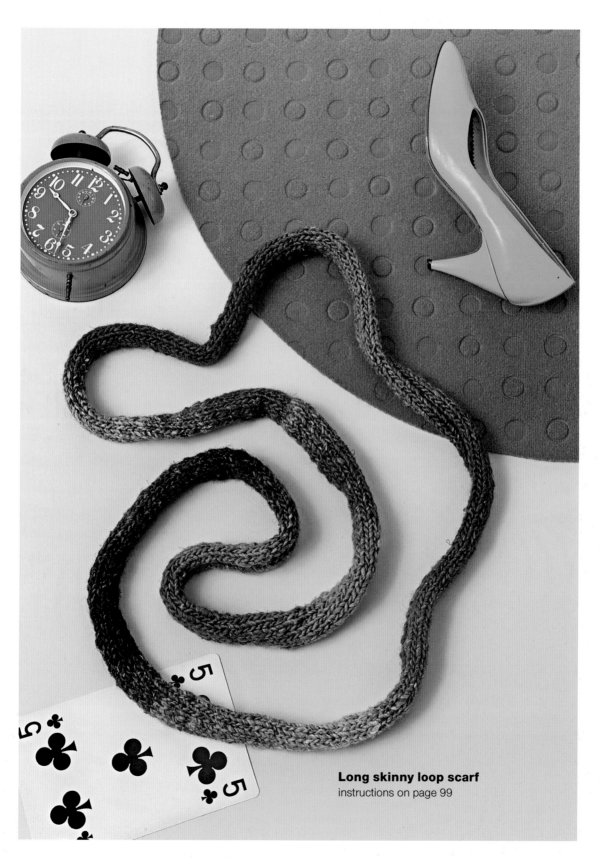

Long skinny loop scarf
instructions on page 99

Simple braided scarf
instructions on page 100

Striped college scarf
instructions on page 101

**Hooded scarf with
Fair Isle border**
instructions on page 102

Snake scarf
instructions on page 104

"Curl a woolly snake around your neck."

Twisted cowl
instructions on page 106

Long lace scarf with braided tassels
instructions on page 107

Bandana cowl
instructions on page 108

Cream capelet
instructions on page 110

Striped cowl
instructions on page 109

"Uber-cool and super-snuggly—think duvet day on the move."

Cable scarf
instructions on page 112

Neck warmer with button fastening

Neck warmer with button fastening
instructions on page 113

Moustache cowl
instructions on page 114

69

Patterns

On the following pages you'll find the knitting patterns and instructions for all of the scarves, cowls, and neck warmers. The knitting needles, yarn, and other items that you need are listed at the beginning of each pattern.

POMPOM SCARF

With its giant fluffy pompoms, this scarf is a great way to make a statement—without much effort. You can make the pompoms with a special pompom maker (but beware; they are addictive!) or can create your own pompom maker with nothing more sophisticated than a sheet of card. Knitted in 100 percent wool, this generously sized scarf is guaranteed to keep you mega-cozy.

Main photograph
See page 10.

Yarn
Rowan Cocoon (80% merino wool, 20% mohair) chunky yarn
2 x 3½oz (100g) balls (126yd/115m) in shade 825 Clay (A)
1 x 3½oz (100g) ball (126yd/115m) in shade 813 Seascape (B)

Needles and equipment
US 10½ (7mm) knitting needles
Yarn sewing needle
A pompom maker to make 4½in (11.5cm) pompoms, or four cardboard circles each measuring 4½in (11.5cm) in diameter with a 2¼in (5.5cm) diameter hole in the center.

Gauge (tension)
14 sts and 16 rows in stockinette (stocking) stitch to a 4-in (10-cm) square on US 10½ (7mm) needles.

Measurements
The finished scarf is 62in (158cm) long and 11½in (29cm) wide.

Abbreviations
See page 126.

For the scarf
Cast on 34 sts in A.
Row 1: Knit.
Row 2: Purl.
Row 3: Knit.
Row 4: Knit.
Rep these 4 rows 47 times more.
Row 193: Knit.
Row 194: Purl.
Row 195: Knit.
Bind (cast) off.

To make up
Gather the short ends of the scarf using the yarn tails left from casting on and binding (casting) off. Using the pompom maker or cardboard circles, make two large pompoms in B, using half the ball for each pompom. Trim the pompoms and use the tails of yarn to sew one to each scarf end.
Weave in all loose ends.

TWIST HEADBAND

When all you need and want is something to keep your ears warm (and your hair in place) on a blustery day, this chunky headband is a speedily knitted solution. I've made this one in a lovely shade of denim blue, because I thought it would go with so many things. And I've added a vintage style brooch to glam it up just a teeny bit. These are such fun to knit—and so quick—I think you'll want to make one to match every item in your winter wardrobe.

Main photograph
See page 12.

Yarn
Lion Brand Wool-Ease (80% acrylic, 20% wool) worsted (Aran) yarn
1 x 3oz (85g) ball (197yd/180m) in shade 114 Denim

Needles and equipment
US 8 (5mm) knitting needles
Yarn sewing needle
Stitch holder

Other materials
A coordinating vintage-style brooch

Gauge (tension)
18 sts and 24 rows in stockinette (stocking) stitch to a 4-in (10-cm) square on US 8 (5mm) needles.

Measurements
The finished headband measures 10½in (27cm) across (unstretched) and is 5in (13cm) wide.

Abbreviations
See page 126.

For the headband
Cast on 28 sts.
Row 1: [K3, p2] to last 3 sts, k3.
Row 2: [P3, k2] to last 3 sts, p3.
Rep rows 1–2, 25 times more.
Row 55: [K3, p2] twice, k3, p1, turn work, leaving rem 14 sts on stitch holder and cont working on 14 sts just worked only.
Next row: K1, p3, [k2, p3] twice.
Next row: [K3, p2] twice, k3, p1.
Next row: K1, p3, [k2, p3] twice.
Rep last 2 rows twice more.
Break yarn.
Transfer sts on holder to the free needle so that the st nearest to the center of the knitting is nearest to the needle point, then transfer the sts on the needle holding the knitting to the stitch holder.

Rejoin yarn to the RS of the work to knit the sts just transferred from stitch holder and work on these sts only.
Next row: P1, k3, [p2, k3] twice.
Next row: P3, [k2, p3] twice, k1.
Rep last 2 rows twice more.
Next row: K2tog, k2, p2, k3, p2, k2, inc; then transfer sts on holder to the free needle so that the st nearest to the outer edge of the knitting is nearest to the needle point, and bringing these sts across the front of the sts just knitted, inc, k2, p2, k3, p2, k2, ssk.
(28 sts)
Next row: [P3, k2] to last 3 sts, p3.
Next row: [K3, p2] to last 3 sts, k3.
Next row: [P3, k2] to last 3 sts, p3.
Rep last 2 rows, 25 times more.
Bind (cast) off.

To make up
Join two short ends of the headband using flat stitch (see page 124).
Weave in all loose ends.
Fasten brooch to center of twist on front of headband.

LONG STRIPED SCARF

A certain TV character has been adorning his retro wardrobe with something a little like this for many a year—and now it's your turn to get in on the act. It's long—so it's not the quickest scarf to knit. But as it's knitted entirely in garter stitch, it's very simple. And so long as you're the patient sort, and you're happy to while away quite a few hours knitting, this could be the perfect project to get your teeth into. I've knitted it in seven shades of the same type of yarn—but if you've got a stash of light worsted (DK) yarns that you're just dying to get rid of, just work it in stripes of your choice. For a scarf of the length shown here, you will need a total of approximately 1250yd/1143m of yarn.

Main photograph
See page 14.

Yarn
Sirdar Country Style DK (40% nylon, 30% wool, 30% acrylic) light worsted (DK) yarn
1 x 1¾oz (50g) ball (170yd/155m) in shade 530 Chocolate (A)
2 x 1¾oz (50g) balls (170yd/155m) in shade 399 Honey (B)
1 x 1¾oz (50g) ball (170yd/155m) in shade 394 Amber (C)
1 x 1¾oz (50g) ball (170yd/155m) in shade 599 Apples (D)
1 x 1¾oz (50g) ball (170yd/155m) in shade 396 Rustic Red (E)
1 x 1¾oz (50g) ball (170yd/155m) in shade 389 Smokey Stone (F)
2 x 1¾oz (50g) balls (170yd/155m) in shade 477 Mink (G)

Needles and equipment
US 6 (4mm) knitting needles
Yarn sewing needle
A medium size crochet hook for attaching the tassels (optional)

Gauge (tension)
22 sts and 28 rows in stockinette (stocking) stitch to a 4-in (10-cm) square on US 6 (4mm) needles.

Measurements
The finished scarf is 3½yd (3.2m) long (excluding tassels) and is 12in (30cm) wide.

Abbreviations
See page 126.

For the scarf

Cast on 50 sts in A.
Knit 10 rows.
Break A and join in B.
Knit 50 rows.
Break B and join in C.
Knit 14 rows.
Break C and join in D.
Knit 10 rows.
Break D and join in E.
Knit 20 rows.
Break E and join in A.
Knit 8 rows.
Break A and join in F.
Knit 44 rows.
Break F and join in G.
Knit 26 rows.
Break G and join in D.
Knit 8 rows.
Break D and join in B.
Knit 34 rows.
Break B and join in E.
Knit 16 rows.

Break E and join in C.
Knit 8 rows.
Break C and join in A.
Knit 12 rows.
Break A and join in G.
Knit 46 rows.
Break G and join in D.
Knit 10 rows.
Break D and join in F.
Knit 18 rows.
Break F and join in E.
Knit 10 rows.
Break E and join in B.
Knit 46 rows.
Break B and join in A.
Knit 10 rows.
Break A and join in G.
Knit 22 rows.
Break G and join in F.
Knit 14 rows.
Break F and join in D.
Knit 8 rows.
Break D and join in E.
Knit 20 rows.
Break E and join in A.
Knit 8 rows.
Break A and join in C.
Knit 40 rows.
Break C and join in B.
Knit 12 rows.
Break B and join in F.

Knit 10 rows.
Break F and join in E.
Knit 24 rows.
Break E and join in D.
Knit 16 rows.
Break D and join in G.
Knit 36 rows.
Break G and join in A.
Knit 8 rows.
Break A and join in B.
Knit 42 rows.
Break B and join in C.
Knit 12 rows.
Break C and join in F.
Knit 22 rows.
Break F and join in E.
Knit 8 rows.
Break E and join in A.
Knit 16 rows.
Break A and join in B.
Knit 8 rows.
Break B and join in D.
Knit 20 rows.
Break D and join in G.
Knit 50 rows.
Break G and join in E.
Knit 12 rows.
Break E and join in F.
Knit 14 rows.
Break F and join in D.
Knit 10 rows.

Break D and join in A.
Knit 26 rows.
Break A and join in C.
Knit 12 rows.
Bind (cast) off.

To make up

For the tassels, cut 39 x 11-in (28-cm) lengths of yarns C and D and cut 36 x 11-in (28-cm) lengths of B and G. For each tassel, hold three strands of yarn together, fold the bundle in half, push the folded end through the knitting, then loop the cut ends through the folded end. In this way, attach 25 tassels along the cast-on edge, alternating yarns C and G and beginning and ending with a tassel in C: you will need to attach a tassel to approximately every other cast-on stitch.
In a similar way, arrange 25 tassels along the bound- (cast-) off edge, alternating yarns D and B, beginning and ending with a tassel in D. Weave in all loose ends.

LACY KNIT NECK WARMER

This unashamedly romantic, snug-fitting neck warmer is the perfect accessory when you need to keep out the cold, but don't want to compromise on girly charm. It's also a great project choice if you've dipped your toe into the world of lacy knitting and are on the lookout for something challenging—but not too hard. And perhaps best of all, you'll only need one ball of deliciously soft and light angora yarn.

Main photograph
See page 16.

Yarn
Rowan Angora Haze (69% angora, 20% polyamide, 11% wool) 4-ply yarn 1 x 1oz (25g) ball (150yd/137m) in shade 527 Kiss

Needles and equipment
US 5 (3.75mm) knitting needles
US 2/3 (3mm) knitting needles
Yarn sewing needle

Gauge (tension)
20 sts and 25 rows in stockinette (stocking) stitch to a 4-in (10-cm) square on US 5 (3.75mm) needles.

Measurements
The finished neck warmer measures 9½in (24cm) across and is 5½in (14cm) deep.

Abbreviations
See page 126.

The neck warmer is knitted in two parts—the main part and the lacy border, which is sewn on.

Main part
Using US 5 (3.75mm) needles, cast on 85 sts.
Row 1: K1, [p1, k1, yo, p2tog, k1, p1, k1] to end.
Row 2: P1, [k2, yo, p2tog, k2, p1] to end.
Rep rows 1–2, 14 times more.
Bind (cast) off.

Border
Using US 2/3 (3mm) needles, cast on 6 sts.
Row 1: K1, k2tog, yo, k2, yo2, k1. *(8 sts)*
Row 2: P1, p into front and back of yo in previous row, p2tog, yo, p3.

Row 3: K1, k2tog, yo, k5.
Row 4: Bind (cast) off 2 sts, p2tog, yo, p3. *(6 sts)*
Rep rows 1–4, 26 times more.
Bind (cast) off.

To make up
Join the border to the bound- (cast-) off edge of the main piece using flat stitch (see page 124).
Using flat stitch, join the back seam.
Weave in all loose ends.

PATCHWORK SCARF

If you love all those scarves made from crochet granny squares, but you have a seriously bad case of crochet-phobia, then this scarf is an absolute must. It features a delicious palette of retro shades, and you have to look closely to see that it's actually knitted—apart from the easy-peasy crochet edging. On top of all that, it is 100% cotton, which means it's ideal for those spring days where there's a bit of a breeze going on. And of course, it's guaranteed to brighten every outfit.

Main photograph
See page 21.

Yarn
Lion Brand Kitchen Cotton (100% cotton) worsted (Aran) yarn
2 x 2oz (57g) balls (99yd/90m) in shade 148 Tropic Breeze (A)
2 x 2oz (57g) balls (99yd/90m) in shade 157 Citrus (B)
2 x 2oz (57g) balls (99yd/90m) in shade 130 Snap Pea (C)
2 x 2oz (57g) balls (99yd/90m) in shade 103 Bubblegum (D)

Needles and equipment
US 8 (5mm) knitting needles
US G-6 (4mm) or similar size crochet hook
Yarn sewing needle

Gauge (tension)
16 sts and 22 rows in stockinette (stocking) stitch to a 4-in (10-cm) square on US 8 (5mm) needles.

Measurements
The finished scarf is 55in (139cm) long and 11½in (29cm) wide.

Abbreviations
See page 126.

For the scarf
Cast on 12 sts in A.
Row 1: K2, [yo, k4] twice, yo, k2.
Row 2: P2tog, *(k1, p1) into the yo of the previous row, [p2tog] twice; rep from * once more, (k1, p1) into the yo of the previous row, p2tog.
Row 3: K4, [yo, k4] twice.
Row 4: P2, p2tog, (k1, p1) into the yo of the previous row, [p2tog] twice, (k1, p1) into the yo of the previous row, p2tog, p2.
Rep rows 1–4, 3 times more.
Row 17: Knit.
Break A and join in B.
Row 18: Purl.

Rep rows 1–17 once more.
Break B and join in C.
Row 36: Purl.
Rep rows 1–17 once more.
Break C and join in D.
Row 54: Purl.
Rep rows 1–17 once more.
Break D and join in A.
Row 72: Purl.
Rep rows 1–72 twice more.
Then rep rows 1–54 once more, followed by rows 1–16 in D.
Bind (cast) off.
Make two more long strips. The second strip should follow the color sequence D, A, B, C. The third strip should follow the color sequence C, D, A, B.

To make up
Arrange the three strips side by side with the first strip on the left, the second in the middle, and the third on the right, making sure that all three of the cast-on edges are along one edge and all three bound- (cast-) off edges are along the other edge. Join the three strips using flat stitch (see page 124). Using the crochet hook and A, work a crochet edging around the entire scarf (see page 125).

ROLL-NECK CAPELET

*If you're after timeless
sophistication, this roll-neck capelet
is the perfect solution. Knitted in a
delicate tweedy yarn, with wool and
alpaca, it will keep you warm
without adding loads of bulky
layers. The cable border is knitted
first and the rest of the capelet is
knitted on afterward—so you
need a bit of knitting experience
and patience to tackle this—but
I promise you it will be worth
the effort!*

Main photograph
See page 18.

Yarn
Rowan Felted Tweed DK (50% wool,
25% alpaca, 25% viscose) light worsted
(DK) yarn
2 x 1¾oz (50g) balls (191yd/175m) in
shade 165 Scree

Needles and equipment
US 5 (3.75mm) knitting needles
US 6 (4mm) knitting needles
Medium cable needle
Yarn sewing needle

Gauge (tension)
22 sts and 30 rows in stockinette
(stocking) stitch to a 4-in (10-cm)
square on US 5 (3.75mm) needles and
24 sts and 32 rows in stockinette
(stocking) stitch to a 4-in (10-cm)
square on US 6 (4mm) needles.

Measurements
The finished capelet measures 20in
(51cm) across the lower edge
(unstretched) and 7¾in (20cm) from
the base of the collar to the lower edge.

Abbreviations
See page 126.

Border
Using US 5 (3.75mm) needles, cast on
15 sts.
Row 1: Knit.
Row 2: P12, k3.
Rep rows 1–2, 4 times more.
Row 11: K3, C12F.
Row 12: P12, k3.
Rep rows 1–12, 25 times more.
Row 313: Knit.
Row 314: P12, k3.
Bind (cast) off.

Main part
Using US 6 (4mm) needles and with RS
of border facing you, pick up and knit
158 sts along garter stitch edge.
Row 1: Knit.
Beg with a knit row, work 30 rows st st.
Row 32: K37, k2tog, k2, ssk, k72,
k2tog, k2, ssk, k37. *(154 sts)*
Row 33: Purl.
Row 34: K36, k2tog, k2, ssk, k70,
k2tog, k2, ssk, k36. *(150 sts)*
Row 35: Purl.
Row 36: K33, [k2tog] twice, k2, [ssk]
twice, k64, [k2tog] twice, k2, [ssk]
twice, k33. *(142 sts)*
Row 37: Purl.
Row 38: K31, [k2tog] twice, k2, [ssk]
twice, k60, [k2tog] twice, k2, [ssk]
twice, k31. *(134 sts)*
Row 39: Purl.
Row 40: K29, [k2tog] twice, k2, [ssk]
twice, k56, [k2tog] twice, k2, [ssk]
twice, k29. *(126 sts)*
Row 41: Purl.
Row 42: K27, [k2tog] twice, k2, [ssk]
twice, k52, [k2tog] twice, k2, [ssk]
twice, k27. *(118 sts)*
Row 43: Purl.

Row 44: K25, [k2tog] twice, k2, [ssk] twice, k48, [k2tog] twice, k2, [ssk] twice, k25. *(110 sts)*
Row 45: Purl.
Row 46: K23, [k2tog] twice, k2, [ssk] twice, k44, [k2tog] twice, k2, [ssk] twice, k23. *(102 sts)*
Row 47: Purl.
Row 48: K21, [k2tog] twice, k2, [ssk] twice, k40, [k2tog] twice, k2, [ssk] twice, k21. *(94 sts)*
Row 49: Purl.
Row 50: K3, [p2, k2] to last 3 sts, p3.
Rep row 50, 38 times more.
Bind (cast off) in rib patt.

To make up

Sew back seam of capelet using mattress stitch (see page 124), remembering that the seam at the top of the roll neck will need to be on the outside of the piece, so that it is concealed when rolled down.
Weave in all loose ends.

PULL-THROUGH SCARF WITH FLOWER

This romantic scarf features a pull-through loop to make sure it fits securely and doesn't come unwound. Wear it to lift a plain outfit or co-ordinate with something lacy. The main scarf is knitted in a gorgeous floaty yarn made from an unusual blend of alpaca and cotton. I've decorated this version with a rose knitted from the same yarn—but you could just as easily knit yours from an oddment of any light and fluffy worsted yarn in the color of your choice.

Main photograph
See page 20.

Yarn
Rowan Alpaca Cotton (72% alpaca, 28% cotton) worsted (Aran) yarn
1 x 1¾oz (50g) ball (148yd/135m) in shade 400 Rice (A)
1 x 1¾oz (50g) ball (148yd/135m) in shade 407 Smoked Salmon (B)
Rowan Cashsoft DK (57% extra fine merino, 33% microfiber, 10% cashmere) light worsted (DK) yarn
1 x 1¾oz (50g) ball (126yd/115m) in shade 509 Lime (C)

Needles and equipment
US 9 (5.5mm) knitting needles
US 5 (3.75mm) knitting needles
Stitch holder
Yarn sewing needle

Gauge (tension)
14 sts and 18 rows in stockinette (stocking) stitch to a 4-in (10-cm) square on US 9 (5.5mm) needles.

Measurements
The scarf measures 34¾in (86cm) long and is 4in (10cm) wide at the narrowest part.

Abbreviations
See page 126.

For the scarf
Using US 9 (5.5mm) needles, cast on 3 sts in A.
Row 1: [Inc] twice, k1. *(5 sts)*
Row 2: Knit.
Row 3: Inc, k2, inc, k1. *(7 sts)*
Row 4: Knit.
Row 5: Inc, k4, inc, k1. *(9 sts)*
Row 6: K4, p1, k4.
Row 7: Inc, k to last 2 sts, inc, k1. *(11 sts)*
Row 8: K4, p3, k4.

Row 9: Inc, k to last 2 sts, inc, k1. *(13 sts)*
Row 10: K3, p to last 3 sts, k3.
Rep rows 9–10, 6 times more. *(25 sts)*
Row 23: Knit.
Row 24: K3, p to last 3 sts, k3.
Rep rows 23–24 twice more.
Row 29: K3, k2tog, k to last 5 sts, ssk, k3. *(23 sts)*
Row 30: K3, p to last 3 sts, k3.
Rep rows 29–30 twice more. *(19 sts)*
Row 35: Knit.
Row 36: K3, p to last 3 sts, k3.
Rep rows 35–36, 40 times more.
Row 117: K5, leave next 9 sts on stitch holder, turn work, cast on 9 sts, turn work again, k to end. (19 sts plus 9 sts on stitch holder)
Continue work on needles only.
Row 118: K3, p to last 3 sts, k3.
Row 119: Knit.
Row 120: K3, p to last 3 sts, k3.
Rep rows 119–120, 3 times more.
Row 127: K3, m1, k to last 3 sts, m1, k3. *(21 sts)*
Row 128: K3, p to last 3 sts, k3.
Rep rows 127–128 twice more. *(25 sts)*
Row 133: Knit.
Row 134: K3, p to last 3 sts, k3.
Rep rows 133–134 twice more.
Row 139: K3, k2tog, k to last 5 sts, ssk, k3. *(23 sts)*
Row 140: K3, p to last 3 sts, k3.

Rep rows 139–140, 5 times more.
(13 sts)

Row 151: K3, k2tog, k to last 5 sts, ssk, k3. *(11 sts)*

Row 152: K4, p3, k4.

Row 153: K3, k2tog, k1, ssk, k3. *(9 sts)*

Row 154: K4, p1, k4.

Row 155: K2, k2tog, k1, ssk, k2. *(7 sts)*

Row 156: Knit.

Row 157: K1, k2tog, k1, ssk, k1. *(5 sts)*

Row 158: Knit.

Row 159: K2tog, k1, ssk. *(3 sts)*

Bind (cast) off.

With WS facing and using US 9 (5.5mm) needles, k9 sts from stitch holder.

Knit 10 rows.

Bind (cast) off.

Rose

(Make 1)

Using US 5 (3.75mm) needles, cast on 67 sts in B.

Row 1: K2tog, k to end. *(66 sts)*

Row 2: Knit.

Rep rows 1–2 once more. *(65 sts)*

Row 7: K2tog, k to end. *(64 sts)*

Row 8: [K2tog] to end. *(32 sts)*

Row 9: Knit.

Row 10: [K2tog] to end. *(16 sts)*

Row 11: Knit.

Row 12: [K2tog] to end. *(8 sts)*

Bind (cast) off.

Leaves

(Make 2)

The leaves are knitted from the bottom to the tip.

Using US 5 (3.75mm) needles, cast on 1 st in C.

Row 1: Inc. *(2 sts)*

Row 2: Purl.

Row 3: [Inc] twice. *(4 sts)*

Row 4: Purl.

Row 5: [Inc, k1] twice. *(6 sts)*

Work 6 rows st st beg with a purl row.

Row 12: P2tog, p2, p2tog. *(4 sts)*

Row 13: Knit.

Row 14: [P2tog] twice. *(2 sts)*

Row 15: K2tog. *(1 st)*

Break yarn and fasten off.

To make up

Oversew the gap by the knitted flap to close it. Fold the flap toward the nearest pointed end and oversew in place along the edge to form a loop. Coil the knitted strip to form the rose and secure with a few stitches. Stitch in place on the pull-through loop of the scarf, taking care not to sew through the loop.

Sew the leaves in place just under the rose.

Weave in all loose ends.

TWEEDY KEYHOLE SCARF

This tweedy scarf is smart enough to co-ordinate with workwear—but also a great choice for weekends in the country. It's an ideal project if you want to give two-color knitting a go because you will not have to run any yarns along the back of your work or up the side. The "keyhole" feature—simply a slot in the knitting—keeps the scarf in place brilliantly. But if you fancy something easier and more traditional, simply continue working the scarf in the main pattern till it reaches the length you want.

Main photograph

See page 22.

Yarn

Lion Brand Wool-Ease Thick & Quick (80% acrylic, 20% wool) worsted (Aran) yarn
1 x 3oz (85g) ball (197yd/180m) in shade 167 Eggplant (A)
1 x 3oz (85g) ball (197yd/180m) in shade 98 Natural Heather (B)

Needles and equipment

US 8 (5mm) knitting needles
Yarn sewing needle
Stitch holder

Gauge (tension)

18 sts and 24 rows in stockinette (stocking) stitch to a 4-in (10-cm) square on US 8 (5mm) needles.

Measurements

The finished scarf is 42in (107cm) long and 7½in (19cm) wide when unfastened.

Abbreviations

See page 126.

For the scarf

Cast on 33 sts in A.
Row 1: Using A, knit.
Row 2: Using B, [k1, sl1] to last st, k1.
Row 3: Using B, [k1, yf, sl1, yb] to last st, k1.
Row 4: Using A, knit.
Row 5: Using A, knit.
Row 6: Using B, k2, [yf, sl1, yb, k1] to last st, k1.
Row 7: Using B, k2, [yf, sl1, yb, k1] to last st, k1.
Row 8: Using A, knit.

Rep rows 1–8, 27 times more.
Break B.
Row 225: Using A, k17, turn and work on these 17 sts only, leaving rem 16 sts on stitch holder.
Next row: Rejoin B and using B, [k1, sl1] to last st, k1.
Next row: Using B, [k1, yf, sl1, yb] to last st, k1.
Next row: Using A, knit.
Next row: Using A, knit.
Next row: Using B, k2, [yf, sl1, yb, k1] to last st, k1.
Next row: Using B, k2, [yf, sl1, yb, k1] to last st, k1.
Next row: Using A, knit.
Next row: Using A, knit.
Next row: Using B, [k1, sl1] to last st, k1.
Next row: Using B, [k1, yf, sl1, yb] to last st, k1.
Next row: Using A, knit.
Next row: Using A, knit.
Next row: Using B, k2, [yf, sl1, yb, k1] to last st, k1.
Next row: Using B, k2, [yf, sl1, yb, k1] to last st, k1.
Next row: Using A, knit.
Next row: Using A, knit.
Next row: Using B, [k1, sl1] to last st, k1.

Next row: Using B, [k1, yf, sl1, yb] to last st, k1.

Next row: Using A, knit.

Break both yarns.

Rejoin A to 16 sts on stitch holder on RS of work, leave 17 sts just worked on stitch holder.

Next row: Using A, inc, k to end. *(17 sts)*

Next row: Using B, [k1, sl1] to last st, k1.

Next row: Using B, [k1, yf, sl1, yb] to last st, k1.

Next row: Using A, knit.

Next row: Using A, knit.

Next row: Using B, k2, [yf, sl1, yb, k1] to last st, k1.

Next row: Using B, k2, [yf, sl1, yb, k1] to last st, k1.

Next row: Using A, knit.

Next row: Using A, knit.

Next row: Using B, [k1, sl1] to last st, k1.

Next row: Using B, [k1, yf, sl1, yb] to last st, k1.

Next row: Using A, knit.

Next row: Using A, knit.

Next row: Using B, k2, [yf, sl1, yb, k1] to last st, k1.

Next row: Using B, k2, [yf, sl1, yb, k1] to last st, k1.

Next row: Using A, knit.

Next row: Using A, knit.

Next row: Using B, [k1, sl1] to last st, k1.

Next row: Using B, [k1, yf, sl1, yb] to last st, k1.

Next row: Using A, knit.

Break yarns and work over all sts for remaining project, rejoining yarns on RS of work as required.

Row 245: Using A, k16, k2tog, k16. *(33 sts).*

Row 246: Using B, k2, [yf, sl1, yb, k1] to last st, k1.

Row 247: Using B, k2, [yf, sl1, yb, k1] to last st, k1.

Row 248: Using A, knit.

Row 249: Using A, knit.

Row 250: Using B, [k1, sl1] to last st, k1.

Row 251: Using B, [k1, yf, sl1, yb] to last st, k1.

Row 252: Using A, knit.

Row 253: Using A, knit.

Row 254: Using B, k2, [yf, sl1, yb, k1] to last st, k1.

Row 255: Using B, k2, [yf, sl1, yb, k1] to last st, k1.

Row 256: Using A, knit.

Rep rows 249–256, 8 times more.

Bind (cast) off pwise.

To make up

Weave in all loose ends.

BOA SCARF

If you want to dress to impress without spending all your evenings curled up knitting, this is quite definitely the project for you. With this specialty yarn, you can create a beautiful ruffled scarf in multi-tonal shades in just a couple of evenings. I've used two balls of yarn to make this version extra long—just because I like it that way. But if you want a shorter scarf, then simply use a single ball.

Main photograph
See page 24.

Yarn
Katia Ondas (100% acrylic) fashion yarn
2 x 3½oz (100g) balls (33yd/31m) in shade 75

Needles and equipment
US 6 (4mm) knitting needles
Yarn sewing needle

Gauge (tension)
No particular gauge (tension) is needed for this project.

Measurements
The finished scarf is 95in (240cm) long and 5½in (14cm) wide.

Abbreviations
See page 126.

For the boa
Using the right-hand needle, pick up 7 threads along the top edge of the yarn to form the cast-on sts, leaving about 1in (2.5cm) between each "stitch."
Knit each row, using the top edge of the yarn only, until you have used up both balls.
Bind (cast) off in the normal way until you have one st rem.
Secure the final stitch by using the yarn sewing needle to pull the whole width of the knitting yarn through this stitch. (If you prefer you can secure the final stitch with a needle and thread.)

To make up
Gently pull the yarn to its maximum width to show off the ruffles to their best. The loose ends of the yarn can be woven through the center of the ruffle to conceal them. To make it easier to do this, first cut down the center of the yarn tails to form two narrower lengths.

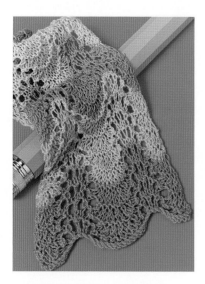

LACE RIPPLE SCARF

If you don't want your scarf to weigh you down, this featherweight scarf knitted in a simple lacy pattern is right up your street. The stitch looks a lot fancier than it is and, once you've had a bit of practice, even beginner knitters will find the pattern well within their grasp. I've knitted this scarf in two shades of soft green, but you could just as easily knit it in one color if you prefer.

Main photograph
See page 26.

Yarn
Debbie Bliss Rialto Lace (100% extra fine merino) lace-weight yarn
1 x 1¾oz (50g) ball (427yd/390m) in shade 25 Sea Green (A)
1 x 1¾oz (50g) ball (427yd/390m) in shade 16 Willow (B)

Needles and equipment
US 8 (5mm) knitting needles
Yarn sewing needle

Gauge (tension)
20 sts and 25 rows in stockinette (stocking) stitch to a 4-in (10-cm) square on US 8 (5mm) needles.

Measurements
The scarf is 63in (160cm) long and 5in (13cm) wide.

Abbreviations
See page 126.

For the scarf
Cast on 38 sts in A.
Row 1: Knit.
Row 2: Purl.
Row 3: K1, *[k2tog] 3 times, [yo, k1] 6 times, [k2tog] 3 times; rep from * to last st, k1.
Row 4: Knit.
Rep rows 1–4, 3 times more.
Join in B, do not break A but carry it up the side of the work.
Row 17: Knit.
Row 18: Purl.
Row 19: K1, *[k2tog] 3 times, [yo, k1] 6 times, [k2tog] 3 times; rep from * to last st, k1.
Row 20: Knit.
Rep rows 17–20, 3 times more.
(32 rows completed)
Rep rows 1–32, 9 times more, carrying the yarn not in use up the side of the work.
Break B.
Cont in A.

Row 321: Knit.
Row 322: Purl.
Row 323: K1, *[k2tog] 3 times, [yo, k1] 6 times, [k2tog] 3 times; rep from * to last st, k1.
Row 324: Knit.
Rep rows 321–322, 3 times more.
Bind (cast) off.

To make up
Weave in all loose ends.

WIDE SCARF

This scarf is the best-ever choice for knitters who want to knit today and wear tomorrow. Even a brand-new knitter can finish this scarf in a couple of days—and if you've got a bit of experience, you can probably knit it in a single evening. The 100 percent wool yarn is thick in some parts and thin in others so creates its own texture. And with the special "dropped" garter stitch, you'll find it grows at a fast pace. Now even the most impatient person has no excuse not to knit.

Main photograph
See page 27.

Yarn
Rowan Thick 'n' Thin (100% wool) super-chunky yarn
4 x 1¾oz (50g) balls (54yd/50m) in shade 968 Dolomite

Needles and equipment
US 15 (10mm) knitting needles
Yarn sewing needle

Gauge (tension)
9 sts and 12 rows in stockinette (stocking) stitch to a 4-in (10-cm) square on US 15 (10mm) needles.

Measurements
The finished scarf is 60½in (153cm) long and 12½in (32cm) wide.

Abbreviations
See page 126.

For the scarf
Cast on 18 sts.
Row 1: Knit, but wind yarn twice around needle on every st.
Row 2: Knit, dropping one loop of every stitch in the previous row.
Rep rows 1–2 till you have used up all your yarn, or the scarf is as long as you want.

To make up
Weave in all loose ends.

RIB SCARF

This beautiful, striped scarf can be worn long and loose, or wrapped around your neck quite a few times. The chunky yarn is the ideal choice for wool-sensitive people, as it's 100% acrylic yet still warm and very soft. And if you want a bit of color without the hassle of chopping and changing yarns, the self-striping feature is sheer perfection. Knitted in a simple rib stitch, it is an ideal first or second project for newbie knitters.

Main photograph
See page 28.

Yarn
Lion Brand Unique (100% acrylic) chunky yarn
4 x 3½oz (100g) balls (109yd/100m) in shade 201 Garden

Needles and equipment
US 10½ (6.5mm) knitting needles
Yarn sewing needle

Gauge (tension)
14 sts and 18 rows to a 4-in (10-cm) square on US 10½ (6.5mm) needles.

Measurements
The scarf is 72in (184cm) long and 12in (30cm) wide.

Abbreviations
See page 126.

For the scarf
Cast on 45 sts.
Row 1: K3, p3 to end.
Row 2: P3, k3 to end.
Rep rows 1 and 2 till you have used up all your yarn, or your scarf is as long as you want it.

To make up
Weave in all loose yarn ends.

WAFFLE-KNIT NECK WARMER

Sweet and beautifully textured, this cozy neck warmer takes just a single ball of soft light worsted (double knitting) yarn. If you put your mind to it, you could whip it up in just a couple of evenings. To keep things romantic, I've added lovely mother of pearl buttons—but you could funk it up a little if the fancy takes you.

Main photograph
See page 30.

Yarn
Jenny Watson Babysoft DK with cashmere (45% extra fine merino, 50% polyamide, 5% cashmere) light worsted (DK) yarn
1 x 1¾oz (50g) ball (120yd/110m) in shade 11

Needles and equipment
US 6 (4mm) knitting needles
Yarn sewing needle
Standard sewing needle

Other materials
3 oval mother-of-pearl buttons, ¾in (2cm) long
Cream sewing thread

Gauge (tension)
22 sts and 28 rows in stockinette (stocking) stitch to a 4-in (10-cm) square on US 6 (4mm) needles.

Measurements
The neck warmer is 23¼in (59cm) long and 4½in (11cm) wide, when unbuttoned.

Abbreviations
See page 126.

For the neck warmer
Cast on 31 sts.
Row 1: K3, [sl1 pwise, k3] to end.
Row 2: K3, [yf, sl1 pwise, yb, k3] to end.
Row 3: K1, [sl1 pwise, k3] to last 2 sts, sl1 pwise, k1.
Row 4: P1, sl1 pwise, [p3, sl1 pwise] to last st, p1.
Rep rows 1–4, 51 times more.
Row 209: K3, make 1 buttonhole (see right), k7, make 1 buttonhole, k7, make 1 buttonhole, k to end.
Knit 2 rows.
Bind (cast) off.

Making the buttonholes
This way of making buttonholes is a little trickier than the standard method where you bind (cast) off the required number of stitches then cast them on again in the following row. But these buttonholes are firmer, which means that your buttons won't slip out unintentionally, and they also look more professional.
Start a buttonhole at the point in your knitting where you want it to be.
Step 1: Yf, sl1, yb, *sl1, pass right slipped st over left slipped st, as if binding (casting) off, and rep from * twice more.
Step 2: Sl 1 st from right-hand needle to left-hand needle.
Step 3: Turn work. Cast on 4 sts using the cable method (see page 118).
Step 4: Turn work. Sl1 then pass the last cast-on stitch over the stitch just slipped. Then pass the stitch onto the left-hand needle.

To make up
Using cream sewing thread, sew the three buttons in position along the side edge of the neck warmer, to align with the buttonholes.
Weave in all loose ends.

MEGA-CHUNKY COWL

When you've got to keep out a serious chill, you'll want something that really looks the business. This cabled cowl, knitted in a stunning tweedy wool, is an absolute winner. I've aimed this version at outdoor types, but different colors will make this style work just as well on those of us who take the great outdoors a little less seriously. The best thing about this scarf, as every knitter knows, is that super-chunky yarn means your knitting grows at a cracking pace!

Main photograph
See page 32.

Yarn
Rowan Drift (100% merino wool) super-chunky yarn
2 x 3½oz (100g) balls (87yd/80m) in shade 908 Shore

Needles and equipment
US 15 (10mm) needles
Medium cable needle
Large-eyed yarn sewing needle

Gauge (tension)
7½ sts and 10 rows in stockinette (stocking) stitch to a 4-in (10-cm) square on US 15 (10mm) needles.

Measurements
The finished cowl measures 16½in (42cm) across and is 11½in (29m) deep.

Abbreviations
See page 126.

For the cowl
Cast on 84 sts.
Row 1: P4, [k6, p8] 5 times, k6, p4.
Row 2: K4, [p6, k8] 5 times, p6, k4.
Row 3: P4, [k6, p8] 5 times, k6, p4.
Row 4: K4, [p6, k8] 5 times, p6, k4.
Row 5: P4, [C6F, p8] 5 times, C6F, p4.
Row 6: K4, [p6, k8] 5 times, p6, k4.
Rep rows 1–6, 4 times more.
Row 31: P4, [k6, p8] 5 times, k6, p4.
Row 32: K4, [p6, k8] 5 times, p6, k4.
Bind (cast) off.

To make up
Join the two short ends using flat stitch (see page 124).
Weave in all loose ends.

FUR COLLAR

If your party outfit needs a bit of a boost, this furry collar with its pompom ties could be just what you're after. The specialty yarn automatically knits up into a silky soft fur that's just begging to be stroked. I've combined the yarn with a matching standard light worsted (double knitting) yarn to make it more substantial and, of course, added those super-cute pompoms.

Main photograph
See page 34.

Yarn
Lion Brand Fun Fur (100% polyester) chunky yarn
1 x 1¾oz (50g) ball (63yd/58m) in shade 124 Champagne (A)
Sublime Baby Cashmere Merino Silk DK (75% extra fine merino, 20% silk, 5% cashmere) light worsted (DK) yarn
1 x 1¾oz (50g) ball (127yd/116m) in shade 359 Sabbia (B)
Sirdar Country Style Wool Blend (40% nylon, 30% wool, 30% acrylic) light worsted (DK) yarn
1 x 1¾oz (50g) ball (170yd/155m) in shade 418 Garnet (C)

Needles and equipment
US 7 (4.5mm) knitting needles
Yarn sewing needle
US G-6 (4mm) or similar size crochet hook
A pompom maker to make 2¼in (5.5cm) pompoms, or four cardboard circles each measuring 2¼in (5.5cm) in diameter with a 1in (2.5cm) diameter hole in the center

Gauge (tension)
13 sts and 20 rows in stockinette (stocking) stitch to a 4-in (10-cm) square on US 7 (4.5mm) needles with yarns A and B knitted together.

Measurements
The finished collar measures 15in (38cm) around the top edge of the neck and is 4½in (11.5cm) deep.

Abbreviations
See page 126.

For the collar
Cast on 118 sts, using yarns A and B together.
Row 1: Inc, k to last 2 sts, inc, k1. *(120 sts)*
Row 2: Inc, p to last 2 sts, inc, k1. *(122 sts)*
Row 3: Inc, k to last 2 sts, inc, k1. *(124 sts)*

Row 4: K2, p to last 2 sts, k2.
Row 5: Knit.
Row 6: K2, p to last 2 sts, k2.
Rep rows 5–6 twice more.
Row 11: K5, [k2tog, k1] 19 times, [k1, ssk] 19 times, k5. *(86 sts)*
Row 12: K2, p to last 2 sts, k2.
Row 13: Knit.
Row 14: K2, p to last 2 sts, k2.
Rep rows 13–14 twice more.
Row 19: K4, [k2tog, k1] 13 times, [k1, ssk] 13 times, k4. *(40 sts)*
Row 20: K2, p to last 2 sts, k2.
Row 21: Knit.
Row 22: K2, p to last 2 sts, k2.
Rep rows 21–22 once more.
Bind (cast) off.

To make up
Using the pompom maker or cardboard circles, make two pompoms in C, using just under ¼oz (6g) for each pompom. Using the crochet hook and B, work two crochet chains (see page 125), each 26in (66cm) long, leaving long yarn tails. Fasten one end of each crochet chain to the top inside edge of the collar and fasten the other ends around the center of a pompom. Weave in all loose ends.

CHUNKY RIBBED COWL

Pull it up a bit... pull it down a bit... fold it over... this has got to be one of the most adaptable pieces of neckwear ever. What's more, it involves no fancy shaping and no fancy stitches. In fact, once you've got started, you could practically knit it in your sleep. And did we mention that it's suitable for teens, men, and women. What's not to like?

Main photograph
See page 36.

Yarn
Debbie Bliss Rialto Chunky (100% merino wool) chunky yarn
3 x 1¾oz (50g) balls (66yd/60m) in shade 19 Aqua

Needles and equipment
US 10½ (6.5mm) knitting needles
Yarn sewing needle

Gauge (tension)
15 sts and 21 rows in stockinette (stocking) stitch to a 4-in (10-cm) square on US 10½ (6.5mm) needles.

Measurements
The cowl is 9in (23cm) wide (unstretched) and 12in (30cm) deep.

Abbreviations
See page 126.

For the cowl
Cast on 102 sts.
Row 1: [K3, p3] to end.
Row 2: [P3, k3] to end.
Rep rows 1–2, 22 times more.
Bind (cast) off in rib pattern.

To make up
Sew the row-end edges of the knitting together using mattress stitch (see page 124). Weave in all loose ends.

LONG SCARF WITH POCKETS

This scarf is a must-have personal insulation system for those days when it's almost too cold to poke a toe outside. It's generously proportioned and there are pockets at each end to keep your hands snug. I've selected two complementary shades—but you could just as easily knit the scarf in one color—or even three or more—if you want something utterly unique. And the stitch is simple enough to work when you want to do something a little more challenging than just watching TV.

Main photograph
See page 38.

Yarn
Lion Brand Wool-Ease (80% acrylic, 20% wool) worsted (Aran) yarn
2 x 3oz (85g) balls (197yd/180m) in shade 191 Violet (A)
2 x 3oz (85g) balls (197yd/180m) in shade 123 Seaspray (B)

Needles and equipment
US 9 (5.5mm) knitting needles
Yarn sewing needle

Other materials
2 x 1½-in (4-cm) natural wooden buttons

Gauge (tension)
16 sts and 22 rows in stockinette (stocking) stitch to a 4-in (10-cm) square on US 9 (5.5mm) needles.

Measurements
The finished scarf is 82½in (210cm) long and 9½in (24cm) wide.

Abbreviations
See page 126.

For the scarf
Cast on 47 sts in A.
Row 1: K3, [p1, k3] to end.
Row 2: K1, [p1, k3] to last 2 sts, p1, k1.
Rep rows 1–2, 46 times more.
Row 95: K3, [p1, k3] to end.
Break A and join in B.
Row 96: K1, [p1, k3] to last 2 sts, p1, k1.
Row 97: K3, [p1, k3] to end.
Rep rows 96–97, 179 times more (or until you have used all three balls of B, ending with a row 97).
Break B and join in A.
Row 456: K1, [p1, k3] to last 2 sts, p1, k1.
Row 457: K3, [p1, k3] to end.
Rep rows 456–457, 46 times more.
Row 550: K1, [p1, k3] to last 2 sts, p1, k1.
Bind (cast) off.

To make up
Lay the scarf down so that the side where the color-change looks neatest is uppermost. Fold up the cast-on and bound- (cast-) off edges so that they are in line with the parts of the scarf where the colors change. Sew the sides of the pocket using matching yarn and flat stitch (see page 124).
Sew the buttons in place on the top part of the pockets using a separated strand of B.
Weave in all loose ends.

LACY RUFFLED SCARF

There's no reason why you can't keep the mood and look romantic when the mercury dips. This soft, ruffled scarf is knitted in a wonderful blend of alpaca and the finest merino yarn. I've chosen a delicate, soft mauve for this version—but the yarn comes in a range of beautiful, gentle shades.

Main photograph
See page 40.

Yarn
Rowan Fine Lace (80% baby suri alpaca, 20% fine merino wool) lace-weight yarn
2 x 1¾oz (50g) balls (437yd/400m) in shade 921 Antique

Needles and equipment
US 8 (5mm) circular knitting needle, at least 32in (80cm) long
Yarn sewing needle

Gauge (tension)
18 sts and 24 rows in stockinette (stocking) stitch to a 4-in (10-cm) square on US 8 (5mm) needles using doubled yarn.

Measurements
The scarf is 79in (200cm) long.

Abbreviations
See page 126.

For the scarf
Cast on 220 sts, using doubled yarn (see page 116).
Knit back and forth on the circular needle, not round and round. So, knit the stitches, transferring them from one tip of the needle to the other tip, then when you reach the end of the row, swap the tips in your hands and work back along the row.
Knit 3 rows.
Row 4: [Inc] to end. *(440 sts)*
Knit 3 rows.
Row 8: [Inc] to end. *(880 sts)*
Knit 3 rows.
Bind (cast) off.

To make up
Weave in all loose ends.

SKINNY LACE SCARF

Fashionably thin, this scarf looks great either wound around your neck to keep you warm or simply hanging loose. It is knitted in a delicate angora yarn and created from two lacy borders that are then sewn together along their long edges to create the ultra-lacy look. Once you've got into the swing of the stitches that create the pattern, it will soon become second nature.

Main photograph
See page 41.

Yarn
Rowan Angora Haze (69% angora, 20% polyamide, 11% wool) 4-ply yarn 2 x 1oz (25g) balls (150yd/137m) in shade 524 Hug

Needles and equipment
US 5 (3.75mm) knitting needles
Yarn sewing needle

Gauge (tension)
20 sts and 25 rows in stockinette (stocking) stitch to a 4-in (10-cm) square on US 5 (3.75mm) needles.

Measurements
The scarf is 55in (140cm) long and 4¼in (11cm) wide.

Abbreviations
See page 126.

For the scarf
(Make 2)
Cast on 10 sts.
Knit 2 rows.
Row 3: K3, [yo, k2tog] twice, yo2, k2tog, k1. *(11 sts)*
Row 4: K3, p1, k2, [yo, k2tog] twice, k1.
Row 5: K3, [yo, k2tog] twice, k1, yo2, k2tog, k1. *(12 sts)*
Row 6: K3, p1, k3, [yo, k2tog] twice, k1.
Row 7: K3, [yo, k2tog] twice, k2, yo2, k2tog, k1. *(13 sts)*
Row 8: K3, p1, k4, [yo, k2tog] twice, k1.
Row 9: K3, [yo, k2tog] twice, k6.
Row 10: Cast off 3 sts (1 st rem on RH needle), k4, [yo, k2tog] twice, k1. *(10 sts)*
Rep rows 3–10, 39 times more.
Knit 2 rows.
Bind (cast) off.

To make up
Join the two pieces together along their straight edges using flat stitch (see page 124). Weave in all loose ends.

CHUNKY CABLE NECK WARMER

Simple but effective is the name of the game for this neck warmer, suitable for the boys and men in your life as well as girls and women. Because it's knitted in a cotton mix, it's ideal for those days when you're not quite sure what the weather will do, as well as for those determinedly chilly days. If you haven't tried cables, here's your chance—they're really much, much easier than you might think.

Main photograph
See page 42.

Yarn
Rowan All Seasons Chunky (60% cotton, 40% acrylic) chunky yarn 2 x 3½oz (100g) balls (93yd/85m) in shade 605 Reach

Needles and equipment
US 10½ (7mm) knitting needles
Medium cable needle
Yarn sewing needle

Gauge (tension)
11 sts and 16 rows in stockinette (stocking) stitch to a 4-in (10-cm) square on US 10½ (7mm) needles.

Measurements
The finished neck warmer is 13in (33cm) across (unstretched) and 6½in (16.5cm) deep.

Abbreviations
See page 126.

For the neck warmer
Cast on 20 sts.
Row 1: P4, k12, p4.
Row 2: K4, p12, k4.
Row 3: P4, k12, p4.
Row 4: K4, p12, k4.
Row 5: P4, C6B, C6F, p4.
Row 6: K4, p12, k4.
Row 7: P4, k12, p4.
Row 8: K4, p12, k4.
Rep rows 3–8, 16 times more.
Row 105: P4, k12, p4.
Row 106: K4, p12, k4.
Row 107: P4, C6B, C6F, p4.
Row 108: K4, p12, k4.
Bind (cast) off.

With RS facing, pick up and k 56 sts along one of the long edges, keeping the gauge (tension) loose.
Next row: Knit.
Bind (cast) off.
Rep along the other long edge.

To make up
Join the two short ends using flat stitch (see page 124).
Weave in all loose ends.

SIMPLE CAPELET

It may surprise you to discover that this stylish capelet is a simple knitted rectangle. What's more, to create it you need know nothing more than how to cast on and bind (cast) off, and how to work the knit and purl stitches. So if you want something that's impressive as well as easy, this is definitely the project for you.

Main photograph
See page 44.

Yarn
Rowan Baby Merino Silk DK (66% wool, 34% silk) light worsted (DK) yarn 2 x 1¾oz (50g) balls (148yd/135m) in shade 686 Cantaloupe

Needles and equipment
US 6 (4mm) knitting needles
Yarn sewing needle

Other materials
1 x 1⅜in (35mm) button in dark red

Gauge (tension)
22 sts and 30 rows in stockinette (stocking) stitch to a 4-in (10cm) square on US 6 (4mm) needles.

Measurements
The finished cape measures 34¼in (87cm) along lower edge and is 8in (20cm) deep.

Abbreviations
See page 126.

For the capelet
Cast on 48 sts.
Knit 2 rows.
Row 3: K4, [k1, p2] to last 5 sts, k5.
Row 4: K4, [p1, k2] to last 5 sts, p1, k4.
Row 5: Knit.
Row 6: K4, p to last 4 sts, k4.
Rep rows 3–6, 56 times more.
Row 231: K4, [k1, p2] to last 5 sts, k5.
Row 232: K4, [p1, k2] to last 5 sts, p1, k4.
Knit 2 rows.
Bind (cast) off.

To make up
Fold down 2¼in (7cm) at the top corners of both ends of the capelet and overlap the right over the left side.
Sew on the button, using the picture as a guide, taking in all the front layers so the two ends are held in place.
Fold down the top edge of the capelet to form the collar.
Weave in all loose ends.

FINE LACE-KNIT CAPELET

Knits definitely aren't just for the winter months. This delicate capelet, knitted in a luxurious feather-light mohair with sparkly sequins, is the perfect accessory for spring and summer evenings, when the heat of the day fades just a little. The capelet is knitted as a simple rectangle—so there's no fancy shaping—and the satin ribbon is simply threaded through the lacy holes along one edge.

Main photograph
See page 46.

Yarn
Rowan Kidsilk Haze Glamour (55% mohair, 22% silk, 20% nylon, 3% polyester) light worsted (DK) yarn 2 x ¾oz (25g) balls (177yd/162m) in shade 281 Majestic

Needles and equipment
US 9 (5.5mm) knitting needles
Yarn sewing needle
Small crochet hook

Other materials
1⅝yd (1.5m) of 1-in (25-mm) wide satin ribbon in teal

Gauge (tension)
20 sts and 26 rows in stockinette (stocking) stitch to a 4-in (10-cm) square on US 9 (5.5mm) needles.

Measurements
The finished capelet is 48½in (123cm) (ungathered) across and 10½in (27cm) long, excluding the scalloped edging.

Abbreviations
See page 126.

For the capelet
Cast on 200 sts.
Row 1: [K2tog, yo, ssk] to end.
Row 2: [P1, (p1, k1) into yo on row below, p1] to end.
Rep rows 1–2, 20 times more.
Row 43: Knit.
Bind (cast) off.

To make up
To make the scallop trim, with RS facing, secure yarn at corner of bound-(cast-) off edge. Using the crochet hook, work a 5-link chain (see page 125), then secure the final link to the lower edge. Continue across the lower edge.
Weave in all yarn ends.
Thread ribbon through holes in first row of knitting to form neck tie.

BANDANA WITH TASSELS

If you're after a relaxed, Bohemian feel, this wide triangular scarf will be a great addition to your wardrobe. It's knitted in a beautifully soft alpaca yarn that has a subtle variegation. The lacy look is slightly deceptive as the stitch is actually a version of seed (moss) stitch. So the only knitting stitches you'll need to know are knit and purl. Best of all perhaps, the scarf will only take one skein of your main yarn to complete. You can make the tassels from an oddment of contrasting yarn in your stash.

Main photograph
See page 48.

Yarn
Rowan Alpaca Colour (100% baby alpaca) light worsted (DK) yarn 1 x 1¾oz (50g) skein (131yd/120m) in shade 138 Ruby (A)
Sublime Extra Fine Merino Wool DK (100% wool) light worsted (DK) yarn 1 x 1¾oz (50g) ball (126yd/116m) in shade 340 Firecracker (B)

Needles and equipment
US 9 (5.5mm) knitting needles
Yarn sewing needle

Gauge (tension)
15 sts and 20 rows in stockinette (stocking) stitch to a 4-in (10cm) square on US 9 (5.5mm) needles in A.

Measurements
The scarf measures 49in (125cm) across the long edge and 8¼in (21cm) from the long edge to the point, excluding tassels.

Abbreviations
See page 126.

For the bandana
Cast on 5 sts in A.
Knit 2 rows.
Row 3: K1, m1, p1, k1, p1, m1, k1. *(7 sts)*
Row 4: K1, m1, [p1, k1] twice, p1, m1, k1. *(9 sts)*
Row 5: K1, m1, [k1, p1] to last 2 sts, k1, m1, k1. *(11 sts)*
Rep row 5 once more. *(13 sts)*
Row 7: K1, m1, [p1, k1] to last 2 sts, p1, m1, k1. *(15 sts)*
Rep row 7 once more. *(17 sts)*
Row 9: Cast on 3 sts, k2, [k1, p1] to last 2 sts, k2. *(20 sts)*

Row 10: Cast on 3 sts, k2, [p1, k1] to last st, k1. *(23 sts)*
Rep rows 9–10, 3 times more. *(41 sts)*
Row 17: Cast on 5 sts, k2, [k1, p1] to last 2 sts, k2. *(46 sts)*
Row 18: Cast on 5 sts, k2, [p1, k1] to last st, k1. *(51 sts)*
Rep rows 17–18, 12 times more. *(171 sts)*
Bind (cast) off.

Tassels
(Make 3)
Using B, wind yarn around the four fingers of your hand about 20 times. Break yarn. Using a 6-in (15-cm) strand of the same yarn, tie it firmly around the yarn loops, ½in (just over 1cm) down from one end. Trim the tassel ends. Thread another 6-in (15-cm) strand of yarn through the loop at one end of the tassel.

To make up
Fasten one tassel to each corner of the scarf.
Weave in all loose ends.

LONG SKINNY LOOP SCARF

This super-easy-to-knit scarf is one big loop, worked in a colorful, luxury, wool and silk mix yarn. You can wind it round your neck twice, three or even four times to create a variety of different looks. The scarf is knitted entirely in stockinette (stocking) stitch—which grows nice and quickly—and the sides curl in naturally. Once you're in the groove, you'll be able to knit it in a single evening.

Main photograph
See page 49.

Yarn
Noro Obi yarn (55% wool, 35% silk, 10% mohair) chunky yarn
1 x 3½oz (100g) skein (175yd/160m) in shade 3

Needles and equipment
US 9 (5.5mm) knitting needles
Yarn sewing needle

Gauge (tension)
14 sts and 21 rows in stockinette (stocking) stitch to a 4-in (10-cm) square on US 9 (5.5mm) needles.

Measurements
The scarf measures 94in (240cm) long before the ends are sewn together.

Abbreviations
See page 126.

For the scarf
Cast on 12 sts.
Beg with a knit row, work in st st until you have used up almost all the yarn.
Bind (cast) off.

To make up
Sew the two short ends of the long strip together using mattress stitch (see page 124).
Weave in all loose ends.

SIMPLE BRAIDED SCARF

Keep your neck warm when the frost strikes with a giant woolly braid. This super-simple scarf looks like you've worked a fancy cable. But in reality, it's just three long strips braided together. The super-chunky yarn knits up in a trice, making it an ideal project for beginners who are after something a little different—and impatient knitters of all levels! I've chosen a delicate shade of cool pale blue for this version, but you can choose any shade you like.

Main photograph
See page 50.

Yarn
Lion Brand Wool-Ease Thick & Quick (82% acrylic, 10% wool, 8% rayon) super-chunky yarn
4 x 6oz (170g) balls (106yd/97m) in shade 105 Glacier

Needles and equipment
US 15 (10mm) knitting needles
Yarn sewing needle

Gauge (tension)
8 sts and 11 rows in stockinette (stocking) stitch to a 4-in (10-cm) square on US 15 (10mm) needles.

Measurements
The finished scarf is 72in (182cm) long and 7in (18cm) wide.

Abbreviations
See page 126.

Strips
(Make 3)
Cast on 10 sts.
Knit 170 rows.
Bind (cast) off.

Tassels
(Make 2)
Cut 30 12-in (30-cm) lengths of yarn and arrange all but two of the lengths in a neat bunch. Tie one of the yarn lengths securely around the middle point of the bunch. Holding the ends of the tie, smooth the cut edges downward. Tie the second length of yarn around the doubled bunch, about 2in (5cm) from the top. Trim the tassel ends.

To make up
Lay the three strips on top of each other and oversew the three short ends together. Braid the strips loosely. Lay the three short free ends one on top of the other and oversew the edges together.
Attach the tassels.
Weave in all loose ends.

STRIPED COLLEGE SCARF

If you're after a true classic, look no further than this stripy scarf. It's knitted in a super-chunky yarn so is extremely quick to knit. Best of all, you'll need to know nothing more than the standard knit stitch to create this mega-cozy number. Knit it in the college or team colors of your choice to ward off the winter chills when you're out and about or watching the game.

Main photograph
See page 52.

Yarn
Rowan Big Wool (100% wool) super-chunky yarn
2 x 3½oz (100g) balls (87yd/80m) in shade 1 White Hot (A)
1 x 3½oz (100g) balls (87yd/80m) in shade 52 Steel Blue (B)

Needles and equipment
US 17 (12mm) circular knitting needle at least 32in (80cm) long
Yarn sewing needle

Gauge (tension)
7.5 sts and 11.5 rows in stockinette (stocking) stitch to a 4-in (10-cm) square on US 17 (12mm) needles.

Measurements
The scarf is 72in (184cm) long and 6in (15.5cm) wide.

Abbreviations
See page 126.

For the scarf
Cast on 145 sts in A.
Knit back and forth on the circular needle, not round and round. So, knit the stitches, transferring them from one tip of the needle to the other tip, then when you reach the end of the row, swap the tips in your hands and work back along the row.
Knit 2 rows in A.
Join in B, do not break A.
Knit 2 rows in B.
Rep these 4 rows 4 times more.
Break B and cont in A.
Knit 2 rows.
Bind (cast) off.

To make up
Weave in all loose ends.

HOODED SCARF WITH FAIR ISLE BORDER

This scarf is for fans of traditional knits with a contemporary twist. Worked in a delicious shade of strawberry red with an easier-than-it-looks Fair Isle style border, the center part of the scarf is sewn together to form a simple hood—although this part is strictly optional. If you're making your first foray into knitting with two colors of yarn at once, the simple pattern on this scarf is a great place to start.

Main photograph
See page 54.

Yarn
Rowan Baby Merino Silk DK (66% wool, 34% silk) light worsted (DK) yarn 3 x 1¾oz (50g) balls (148yd/135m) in shade 687 Strawberry (A)
Debbie Bliss Rialto DK (100% wool) light worsted (DK) yarn 1 x 1¾oz (50g) ball (115yd/105m) in shade 002 Ecru (B)

Needles and equipment
US 6 (4mm) knitting needles
Yarn sewing needle
Medium-sized crochet hook for attaching tassels (optional)

Gauge (tension)
22 sts and 30 rows in stockinette (stocking) stitch to a 4-in (10-cm) square on US 6 (4mm) needles.

Measurements
The finished scarf is 54½in (138cm) long (before folding and stitching the hood part) and 10¼in (26cm) wide.

Abbreviations
See page 126.

For the scarf
Cast on 53 sts in A.
Row 1: Knit.
Row 2: Knit.
Row 3: K2, p to last 2 sts, k2.
Rep rows 2–3 once more.
Row 6: K3, drop A and join in B, (k1 in B, k1 in A) to last 2 sts, k2 in A.
Row 7: K2 in A, break A, p in B to last 2 sts, rejoin A and k2.
Row 8: K3 in A, (k1 in B, k1 in A) to last 2 sts, k2 in A.

Break B and cont in A only.
Work 3 rows in st st, beg with a purl row and remembering to k 2 sts at beg and end of every WS row.
Join in yarn B.
Work motif from chart opposite.
Break B and cont in A only.
Work 3 rows in st st, beg with a purl row and remembering to k 2 sts at beg and end of every WS row.
Row 28: K3 in A, drop A and join in B, (k1 in B, k1 in A) to last 2 sts, k2 in A.
Row 29: K2 in A, break A, p in B to last 2 sts, rejoin A and k2.
Row 30: K3 in A, (k1 in B, k1 in A) to last 2 sts, k2 in A.
Break B and cont in A only.
Work 245 rows in st st beg with a purl row and remembering to k 2 sts at beg and end of every WS row.
Row 276: K3 in A, drop A and join in B, (k1 in B, k1 in A) to last 2 sts, k2 in A.
Row 277: K2 in A, break A, p in B to last 2 sts, rejoin A and k2.
Row 278: K3 in A, (k1 in B, k1 in A) to last 2 sts, k2 in A.
Break B and cont in A only.
Work 3 rows in st st beg with a purl row and remembering to k 2 sts at beg and end of every WS row.

Work motif from chart below.

Break B and cont in A only.

Work 3 rows in st st beg with a purl row and remembering to k 2 sts at beg and end of every WS row.

Row 298: K3 in A, drop A and join in B, (k1 in B, k1 in A) to last 2 sts, k2 in A.

Row 299: K2 in A, break A, p in B to last 2 sts, rejoin A and k2.

Row 300: K3 in A, (k1 in B, k1 in A) to last 2 sts, k2 in A.

Break B and cont in A only.

Work 4 rows in st st beg with a purl row and remembering to k 2 sts at beg and end of every WS row.

Next row: Knit.

Bind (cast) off.

To make up

For the tassels, cut 208 12-in (30-cm) lengths of B. Arrange the lengths in 52 groups of four yarn lengths. For each tassel, fold the group in half, push the folded end through the knitting, then loop the cut ends through the folded end. Make 26 evenly spaced tassels along both short edges of the scarf. You can leave the scarf just like this or you can make a little hood. To do this, fold the scarf in half widthways and sew up 9in (23cm) from the fold on one side, using mattress stitch (page 124). Weave in all loose ends.

key to colors

Strawberry (A) ■

Ecru (B) □

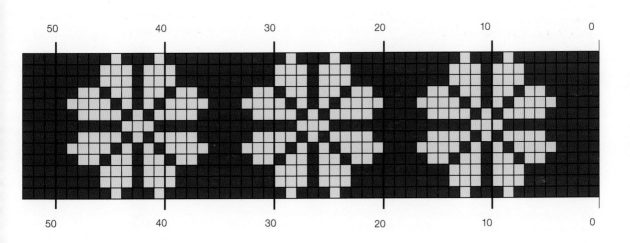

SNAKE SCARF

*If you want to make sure the child in
your life looks cool but stays warm,
check out this woolly snake and
curl it around his or her neck. I've
chosen a lovely olive green for this
snake, and worked a simple
diamond pattern along the top. But
this creature is more than up to a
bit of customization—knit him plain
if you prefer, or try him in stripes
and bust that stash of knitting yarn.
And if you want him a little bit
longer... get hold of another ball of
your basic shade and carry on
knitting for a bit.*

Main photograph
See page 56.

Yarn
Lion Brand Wool-Ease (80% acrylic,
20% wool) worsted (Aran) yarn
2 x 3oz (85g) balls (197yd/180m) in
shade 174 Avocado (A)
1 x 3oz (85g) ball (197yd/180m) in
shade 99 Fisherman (B)
Sirdar Country Style DK (40% nylon,
30% wool, 30% acrylic) light worsted
(DK) yarn
Very small amount in shade 418
Garnet (C)

Needles and equipment
US 8 (5mm) knitting needles
US 5 (3.75mm) knitting needles
Yarn sewing needle

Other materials
2 x ⅞-in (22-mm) brown buttons

Gauge (tension)
18 sts and 24 rows in stockinette
(stocking) stitch to a 4-in (10-cm)
square on US 8 (5mm) needles.

Measurements
The finished scarf is 40½in (103cm)
long (excluding tongue) and 6in
(17cm) wide.

Abbreviations
See page 126.

The two scarf pieces are knitted from
the tail end to the head end.

Top
Using US 8 (5mm) needles, cast on
13 sts in A.
Row 1: Inc, k to last 2 sts, inc, k1.
(15 sts)
Row 2: Purl.
Rep rows 1–2, 10 times more*. *(25 sts)*

Row 23: Inc, k11 in A, k1 in B, k10, inc,
k1 in A. *(27 sts)*
Row 24: P12 in A, k3 in B, p12 in A.
Row 25: Inc, k10 in A, k5 in B, k9, inc,
k1 in A. *(29 sts)*
Row 26: P11 in A, p1 in B, p1 in A, p3
in B, p1 in A, p1 in B, p11 in A.
Row 27: Inc, k9 in A, k3 in B, k1 in A,
k1 in B, k1 in A, k3 in B, k8, inc, k1 in
A. *(31 sts)*
Row 28: P10 in A, p5 in B, p1 in A, p5
in B, p in A to end.
Row 29: K11 in A, k3 in B, k1 in A, k1
in B, k1 in A, k3 in B, k in A to end.
Row 30: P12 in A, p1 in B, p1 in A, p3
in B, p1 in A, p1 in B, p in A to end.
Row 31: K13 in A, k5 in B, k in A
to end.
Row 32: P14 in A, p3 in B, p in A
to end.
Row 33: K15 in A, k1 in B, k in A
to end.
Row 34: Purl in A.
Rows 35–45: Work from chart
opposite.
Row 46: Purl in A.
Rep rows 35–46, 15 times more.
Beg with a knit row, work 6 rows in
st st.
Row 233: K2, k2tog, k to last 4 sts, ssk,
k2. *(29 sts)*
Row 234: Purl.

Rep rows 233–234, 3 times more.
(23 sts)
Row 241: K2, k2tog, k to last 4 sts, ssk, k2. *(21 sts)*
Row 242: P2tog, p to last 2 sts, p2tog. *(19 sts)*
Rep rows 241–242 twice more. *(11 sts)*
Row 247: [K2tog] twice, k3, [ssk] twice. *(7 sts)*
Row 248: P2tog, p3, p2tog. *(5 sts)*
Bind (cast) off.

Underside

Work as for top to *.
Row 23: Inc, k to last 2 sts, inc, k1. *(27 sts)*
Row 24: Purl.
Rep rows 23–24 twice more. *(31 sts)*

Work 210 rows in st st beg with a knit row.
Row 233: K2, k2tog, k to last 4 sts, ssk, k2. *(29 sts)*
Row 234: Purl.
Rep rows 233–234, 3 times more. *(23 sts)*
Row 241: K2, k2tog, k to last 4 sts, ssk, k2. *(21 sts)*
Row 242: P2tog, p to last 2 sts, p2tog. *(19 sts)*
Rep rows 241–242 twice more. *(11 sts)*
Row 247: (K2tog) twice, k3, [ssk] twice. *(7 sts)*
Row 248: P2tog, p3, p2tog. *(5 sts)*
Bind (cast) off.

Tongue

Using US 5 (3.75mm) needles, cast on 24 sts in C.
Bind (cast) off.

To make up

Join the top and underside pieces together using mattress stitch (see page 124).
Stitch the buttons in place for the eyes using a separated strand of B.
Fold the tongue in half widthways and stitch the center point to the mouth.
Weave in all loose ends.

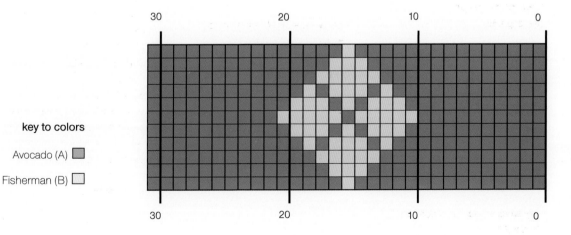

key to colors

Avocado (A) ■

Fisherman (B) □

TWISTED COWL

It's simple, colorful, and sweet. It's knitted entirely in garter stitch—the simplest of all stitches. And it only takes a couple of balls of yarn to complete. So now, not even the youngest and newest of knitters has any excuse not to get clicking. The yarn is variegated or "self striping"—so it creates its own stripes without you having to chop and change between balls of different colors. And remember, you can wear the finished cowl as we've shown here, or around your shoulders, so it's more like a capelet.

Main photograph
See page 58.

Yarn
Lion Brand Amazing (53% wool, 47% acrylic) worsted (Aran) yarn
2 x 1¾oz (50g) balls (147yd/135m) in shade 220 Carnival

Needles and equipment
US 9 (5.5mm) knitting needles
Yarn sewing needle

Gauge (tension)
16 sts and 22 rows in stockinette (stocking) stitch to a 4-in (10-cm) square on US 9 (5.5mm) needles.

Measurements
The finished cowl measures 17in (43cm) across (unstretched) and is 15in (38cm) deep.

Abbreviations
See page 126.

For the cowl
Cast on 56 sts.
Work in garter stitch for 152 rows or until you have almost used up both balls of yarn (leaving enough to sew the ends together.)
Bind (cast) off.

To make up
Twist your knitting once, widthways.
Sew up the two short ends using flat stitch (see page 124).
Weave in all loose ends.

LONG LACE SCARF WITH BRAIDED TASSELS

The wool and mohair yarn and the lacy texture make sure that this scarf is light but still beautifully warm. We love the swingy, braided tassels on the end, which help keep the scarf in place as well as looking lovely. I've knitted this version in various leaf-fall shades. But in cooler colors, it would be brilliant for the slightly chilly days of early spring. The choice, as always, is completely up to you.

Main photograph
See page 59.

Yarn
Rowan Kid Classic (70% wool, 22% mohair, 8% polyamide) light worsted (DK) yarn
1 x 1¾oz (50g) ball (153yd/140m) in shade 870 Rosewood (A)
3 x 1¾oz (50g) balls (153yd/140m) in shade 881 Ochre (B)
1 x 1¾oz (50g) ball (153yd/140m) in shade 872 Earth (C)

Needles and equipment
US 9 (5.5mm) knitting needles
Yarn sewing needle

Gauge (tension)
18 sts and 24 rows in stockinette (stocking) stitch to a 4-in (10-cm) square on US 9 (5.5mm) needles.

Measurements
The finished scarf is 71¼in (181cm) long (excluding braided tassels) and 8¾in (22.5cm) wide.

Abbreviations
See page 126.

For the scarf
Cast on 42 sts in A.
Row 1: Sl1, k2, [yo, skpo, k2] to last 3 sts, yo, skpo, k1.
Row 2: Sl1, p2, [yo, p2tog, p2] to last 3 sts, yo, p2tog, k1.
Rep rows 1–2, 20 times more.
Break A and join in B.
Row 43: Sl1, k2, [yo, skpo, k2] to last 3 sts, yo, skpo, k1.
Row 44: Sl1, p2, [yo, p2tog, p2] to last 3 sts, yo, p2tog, k1.
Rep rows 43–44, 102 times more.
Break B and join in A.
Row 249: Sl1, k2, [yo, skpo, k2] to last 3 sts, yo, skpo, k1.
Row 250: Sl1, p2, [yo, p2tog, p2] to last 3 sts, yo, p2tog, k1.
Rep rows 249–250, 20 times more.
Bind (cast) off.

To make up
For the braided tassels, cut 90 18-in (46-cm) lengths of B and 108 18-in (46-cm) lengths of C. Arrange the lengths of B into 10 groups, each containing nine lengths of yarn. Arrange the lengths of C into 12 groups, each containing nine lengths of yarn. Thread a group of C lengths of yarn through one corner of a short side of the scarf and divide the ends of the yarn into three groups, each containing six lengths. Braid the yarn to within 2in (5cm) of the end of the lengths, then tie two ends around the braid to secure. Repeat this process across the short side of the scarf in alternate colors, so that you have a total of 11 tassels, beginning and ending with a tassel in C. Repeat for the other short end of the scarf. Trim ends. Weave in all loose ends.

BANDANA COWL

For an urban take on cute cowboy chic, knit the toddler in your life this neck-warming bandana cowl, complete with subtle spot pattern. We've knitted it in a soft but slightly zingy lime that would suit either a girl or boy—but you can of course knit it in whatever shade takes your fancy. It uses just one ball of yarn, so you may find that you want to knit one to suit every outfit.

Main photograph
See page 60.

Yarn
Sublime Baby Cashmerino Silk DK (75% extra fine merino wool, 20% silk, 5% cashmere) light worsted (DK) yarn 1 x 1¾oz (50g) ball (127yd/116m) in shade 195 Puzzle

Needles and equipment
US 6 (4mm) knitting needles
Yarn sewing needle

Gauge (tension)
22 sts and 28 rows in stockinette (stocking) stitch to a 4-in (10-cm) square on US 6 (4mm) needles.

Measurements
The bandana cowl is 6½in (16.5cm) wide at the top and 8½in (22cm) long from the neck edge to the pointed lower edge. It should fit an average-size child of 1–3 years.

Abbreviations
See page 126.

For the bandana
Cast on 73 sts.
Beg with a knit row, work 2 rows in st st.
Row 3: P1, [k3, p1] to end.
Beg with a purl row, work 3 rows in st st.
Row 7: K2, p1, [k3, p1] to last 2 sts, k2.
Beg with a purl row, work 3 rows in st st.
Rep rows 3–10 twice more.
Row 27: K20, [p1, k3] 8 times, p1, k20.
Row 28: K19, p35, k to end.
Row 29: Knit.
Row 30: K19, p35, k to end.
Row 31: Bind (cast) off 16 sts (1 st rem on needle), k5, [p1, k3] 8 times, k3, bind (cast) off rem 16 sts. *(41 sts)*
Break yarn and rejoin it to WS of work.
Row 32: K3, ssk, p to last 5 sts, k2tog, k3. *(39 sts)*
Row 33: K3, k2tog, k to last 5 sts, ssk, k3. *(37 sts)*

Row 34: K3, ssk, p to last 5 sts, k2tog, k3. *(35 sts)*
Row 35: K3, k2tog, [p1, k3] to last 6 sts, p1, ssk, k3. *(33 sts)*
Rep rows 32–34 once more. *(27 sts)*
Row 39: K3, k2tog, k2, [p1, k3] to last 8 sts, p1, k2, ssk, k3. *(25 sts)*
Row 40: K3, p to last 3 sts, k3.
Row 41: K3, k2tog, k to last 5 sts, ssk, k3. *(23 sts)*
Row 42: K3, p to last 3 sts, k3.
Rep rows 39–42 twice more. *(15 sts)*
Row 51: K3, k2tog, k2, p1, k2, ssk, k3. *(13 sts)*
Row 52: K3, p to last 3 sts, k3.
Row 53: K3, k2tog, k3, ssk, k3. *(11 sts)*
Row 54: K3, p5, k3.
Row 55: K3, k2tog, k1, ssk, k3. *(9 sts)*
Row 56: K3, p3, k3.
Row 57: K2, k2tog, k1, ssk, k2. *(7 sts)*
Row 58: K3, p1, k3.
Row 59: K1, k2tog, k1, ssk, k1. *(5 sts)*
Row 60: Knit.
Row 61: K2tog, k1, ssk. *(3 sts)*
Row 62: Sl1, k2tog, psso. *(1 st)*
Break yarn and fasten off.

To make up
Sew the back seam of the bandana cowl using mattress stitch (see page 124).
Weave in all loose ends.

STRIPED COWL

There's nothing much nicer than striped neckwear—it always looks chic and is always in fashion. This cowl, knitted entirely in garter stitch, is very straightforward to make. I've chosen cool shades of pale blue and white for mine, but vibrant, clashing shades would also be brilliant. I've added a simple scalloped trim—much easier to work than it looks, but you can leave yours plain to make your project even simpler. As always, it is completely up to you.

Main photograph
See page 62.

Yarn
Sublime Extra Fine Merino Wool DK (100% extra fine merino) light worsted (DK) yarn
1 x 1¾oz (50g) ball (127yd/116m) in shade 307 Julep (A)
1 x 1¾oz (50g) ball (127yd/116m) in shade 3 Alabaster (B)

Needles and equipment
US 6 (4mm) knitting needles
US 5 (3.75mm) knitting needles
Yarn sewing needle

Gauge (tension)
22 sts and 28 rows in stockinette (stocking) stitch to a 4-in (10-cm) square on US 6 (4mm) needles.

Measurements
The finished cowl measures 10½in (27cm) across (unstretched) and is 8½in (22cm) deep (excluding trim). It should fit an average–size child of 5–10 years.

Abbreviations
See page 126.

For the cowl
Using US 6 (4mm) needles, cast on 98 sts in A.
Row 1: Knit.
Rep row 1, 4 times more.
Leave A at side of work and join in B.
Row 5: Knit.
Rep row 5 once more.
Rep rows 1–6, 9 times more
Rep rows 1–4 once more.
Bind (cast) off.

Lace edging
Using US 5 (3.75mm) needles, cast on 4 sts in B.
Row 1: Sl1, k3.
Row 2: Sl1, k3.
Row 3: Inc, cast on 6 sts onto RH needle (11 sts in total), bind (cast) off 7 sts, turn, k to end. *(4 sts)*
Row 4: Sl1, k3.
Rep row 4, 4 times more.
Row 9: Put right-hand needle through last 2 strands of last cast-on/bound-(cast-) off stitch from row 3, knit into first st on left-hand needle, pass slipped strands over knitted st, knit to end.
Row 10: Sl1, k3.
Rep rows 1–10, 16 times more.
Row 171: Knit.
Bind (cast) off.

To make up
Slip-stitch edging in place along bound-(cast-) off edge of work using B.
Join the two short edges of the cowl using flat stitch (see page 124).
Weave in all loose ends.

CREAM CAPELET

For old-fashioned charm with a bang-up-to-date twist, this charming girl's capelet will keep out the chill and complement all manner of outfits. It is knitted in one piece and features a lovely scalloped edge which involves nothing more than a bit of fancy binding (casting) off. I love the perpetual appeal of simple cream—but if you want something a little bolder, please feel free.

Main photograph
See page 61.

Yarn
Debbie Bliss Cashmerino Aran (55% wool, 33% acrylic, 12% cashmere) worsted (Aran) yarn
3 x 1¾oz (50g) balls (98yd/90m) in shade 101 Ecru (A)
Sirdar Country Style DK (40% nylon, 30% wool, 30% acrylic) light worsted (DK) yarn
1 x 1¾oz (50g) ball (141yd/155m) in shade 471 Pansy (B)

Needles and equipment
US 8 (5mm) knitting needles
US 6 (4mm) knitting needles
Yarn sewing needle

Other materials
One small oval or round white button

Gauge (tension)
16 sts and 26 rows in stockinette (stocking) stitch to a 4-in (10-cm) square on US 8 (5mm) needles in A.

Measurements
The capelet is 7in (18cm) long from the neck to the lower edge and 13¾in (35cm) wide at the lower edge. It should fit an average-size girl of 4–6 years.

Abbreviations
See page 126.

For the capelet
Using US 8 (5mm) needles, cast on 60 sts in A.
Beg with a knit row, work 2 rows in st st.
Row 3: K14, m1, k2, m1, k28, m1, k2, m1, k to end. *(64 sts)*
Row 4 and every WS row: Purl.
Row 5: K15, m1, k2, m1, k30, m1, k2, m1, k to end. *(68 sts)*
Row 7: K16, m1, k2, m1, k32, m1, k2, m1, k to end. *(72 sts)*
Row 9: K17, m1, k2, m1, k34, m1, k2, m1, k to end. *(76 sts)*
Row 11: K18, m1, k2, m1, k36, m1, k2, m1, k to end. *(80 sts)*

Row 13: K19, m1, k2, m1, k38, m1, k2, m1, k to end. *(84 sts)*
Row 15: K20, m1, k2, m1, k40, m1, k2, m1, k to end. *(88 sts)*
Row 17: K21, m1, k2, m1, k42, m1, k2, m1, k to end. *(92 sts)*
Row 19: K22, m1, k2, m1, k44, m1, k2, m1, k to end. *(96 sts)*
Row 21: K23, m1, k2, m1, k46, m1, k2, m1, k to end. *(100 sts)*
Row 23: K24, m1, k2, m1, k48, m1, k2, m1, k to end. *(104 sts)*
Row 25: K25, m1, k2, m1, k50, m1, k2, m1, k to end. *(108 sts)*
Row 27: K26, m1, k2, m1, k52, m1, k2, m1, k to end. *(112 sts)*
Row 29: K27, m1, k2, m1, k54, m1, k2, m1, k to end. *(116 sts)*
Row 31: K28, m1, k2, m1, k56, m1, k2, m1, k to end. *(120 sts)*
Row 32: Purl.
Beg with a knit row, work 2 rows in st st.
Row 35: K27, k2tog, k2, ssk, k54, k2tog, k2, ssk, k to end. *(116 sts)*
Beg with a purl row, work 3 rows in st st.
Row 39: K26, k2tog, k2, ssk, k52, k2tog, k2, ssk, k to end. *(112 sts)*
Beg with a purl row, work 4 rows in st st.
Bind (cast) off to create a scalloped edge: bind (cast) off 1 st, *slip st rem from binding (casting) off onto left-hand needle, cast on 2 sts, bind (cast) off 4 sts, rep from * till there are 2 sts rem on needle. Bind (cast) off rem 2 sts.

First side of collar

With WS facing, pick up and k
30 sts from side of neck edge to
center of capelet.
Knit 13 rows.
Bind (cast) off.

Second side of collar

With WS facing, pick up and
k 30 sts from center of neck
edge to side of capelet.
Knit 13 rows.
Bind (cast) off.

Lower flower petals

Using US 6 (4mm) needles, cast on
15 sts in B.
Next row: K3, turn and work on these
3 sts only.
* Beg with a purl row, work 11 rows in
st st.
Next row: Bind (cast) off 2 sts (1 st
rem on needle).
Next row: Knit into next st on left-hand
needle, then bind (cast) off 1 st and
k2.* *(3 sts)*
Rep from * to * 3 times more.
Beg with a purl row, work 11 rows in st st.
Next row: Bind (cast) off 2 sts (1 st
rem on needle).
Next row: Pick up and k into cast-on
edge on the left-hand side of the base
of the petal. *(2 sts)*
Bind (cast) off rem sts, break yarn, and
fasten off.

Upper flower petals

Using US 6 (4mm) needles, cast on 10 sts
in B.
Next row: K2, turn and work on these
2 sts only.
**Beg with a purl row, work 7 rows in
st st.
Next row: Bind (cast) off 1 st (1 st rem
on needle).
Next row: K into next st on left-hand
needle, then bind (cast) off 1 st and k1.**
(2 sts)
Rep from ** to ** 3 times more.
Beg with a purl row, work 7 rows in st st.
Next row: Bind (cast) off 1 st (1 st rem
on needle).
Next row: Pick up and k into cast-on
edge on the left-hand side of the base
of the petal. *(2 sts)*
Bind (cast) off rem sts, break yarn, and
fasten off.

To make up

Join back seam, including collar, using
mattress stitch (see page 124).
Join the two rows of petals into circles.
Place the smaller circle of petals on the
larger one and stitch together. Stitch the
button in place in the center.
Weave in all loose ends.

CABLE SCARF

For those days when you want to tuck yourself away from the world in something super-thick and snuggly—think duvet day on the move—this scarf is ideal. If you're just getting used to cables, it's the perfect challenge—not too simple but those big needles really help you see what you're doing. And of course, big needles and not too many stitches to cast on means that your creation grows nice and quickly.

Main photograph
See page 64.

Yarn
Lion Brand Wool-Ease Thick & Quick (80% acrylic, 20% wool) super-chunky yarn
1 x 6oz (170g) ball (108yd/98m) in shade 138 Cranberry (A)
2 x 6oz (170g) balls (108yd/98m) in shade 136 Apricot (B)

Needles and equipment
US 15 (10mm) knitting needles
Large cable needle
Yarn sewing needle

Gauge (tension)
8 sts and 11 rows in stockinette (stocking) stitch to a 4-in (10-cm) square on US 15 (10mm) needles.

Measurements
The finished scarf is 72½in (184cm) long and 6¼in (16cm) wide.

Abbreviations
See page 126.

For the scarf
Cast on 21 sts in A.
Beg with a knit row, work 6 rows in st st.
Row 7: K3, [C6F] 3 times.
Beg with a purl row, work 3 rows in st st.
Row 11: [C6B] 3 times, k3.
Row 12: Purl.
Break A and join in B.
Beg with a knit row, work 2 rows in st st.
Row 15: K3, [C6F] 3 times.
Beg with a purl row, work 3 rows in st st.
Row 19: [C6B] 3 times, k3.
Beg with a purl row, work 3 rows in st st.
Rep rows 15–22 (last 8 rows), 19 times more.
Row 175: K3, [C6F] 3 times.

Row 176: Purl.
Break B and join in A.
Beg with a knit row, work 2 rows in st st.
Row 179: [C6B] 3 times, k3.
Beg with a purl row, work 3 rows in st st.
Row 183: K3, [C6F] 3 times.
Beg with a purl row, work 7 rows in st st.
Bind (cast) off.

To make up
Weave in all loose ends.

NECK WARMER WITH BUTTON FASTENING

This quick-to-knit neck warmer, suitable for both girls and boys, is a great choice for knitters wanting something classic, but a little different, and that won't take a month of Sundays to complete. It's knitted in a light worsted (DK) yarn and, because the yarn is used double, your knitting will grow much faster than you think. I've chosen delicate mother-of-pearl buttons for this version—but more colorful or chunkier buttons would work just as well.

Main photograph
See page 66.

Yarn
Rowan Felted Tweed DK (50% wool, 25% alpaca, 25% viscose) light worsted (DK) yarn
1 x 1¾oz (50g) ball (191yd/175m) in shade 184 Celadon

Needles and equipment
US 10 (6mm) knitting needles
Medium cable needle
Standard sewing needle

Other materials
Cream sewing thread
3 x ¾-in (18-mm) mother-of-pearl buttons

Gauge (tension)
14 sts and 18 rows in stockinette (stocking) stitch to a 4-in (10-cm) square on US 10 (6mm) needles, using yarn double (see page 116).

Measurements
The finished neck warmer measures 9½in (24cm) across when buttoned up (unstretched) and is 6¾in (17cm) deep.

Abbreviations
See page 126.

For the neck warmer
Using yarn double, cast on 62 sts.
Row 1: Knit.
Row 2: K2, [p1tbl, k1, p1tbl, k2] to end.
Row 3: P2, [k1tbl, p1, k1tbl, p2] to end.
Row 4: K2, [p1tbl, k1, p1tbl, k2] to end.
Row 5: P2, [sl2 sts onto cable needle and hold in front, k1tbl, slip left st on cable needle onto left-hand needle and p it then k1tbl from cable needle, p2] to end.
Rep rows 2–5, 6 times more.
Row 30: K2, [p1tbl, k1, p1tbl, k2] to end.
Row 31: P2, [k1tbl, p1, k1tbl, p2] to end.
Bind (cast) off.

With RS facing, pick up and k 27 sts along one short edge.
Knit 3 rows.
Row 4: K7, bind (cast) off 1 st (8 sts on needle), k4, bind (cast) off 1 st (13 sts on needle), k4, bind (cast) off 1 st (18 sts on needle), k to end. *(24 sts)*
Row 5: K6, inc, k4, inc, k4, inc, k to end. *(27 sts)*
Knit 2 rows.
Bind (cast) off.
With RS facing, pick up and k 27 sts along second short edge.
Knit 7 rows.
Bind (cast) off.

To make up
Using cream thread, sew buttons in place so that they correspond to the buttonholes.
Weave in all loose ends.

MOUSTACHE COWL

Every self-respecting person is sporting some kind of moustache these days. So what better than to create your own knitted version? Pull it up for that moustachioed look—or leave it down if you prefer. The main snood is knitted from a lovely soft yarn that's comfortable for even the most sensitive skins. The moustache itself is knitted from a small amount of fluffy super-chunky yarn—but you could use two or three strands of thinner yarn if you have a handy oddment.

Main photograph
See page 68.

Yarn
Rowan All Seasons Chunky (60% cotton, 40% acrylic) chunky yarn 1 x 3½oz (100g) ball (93yd/85m) in shade 601 Pebble (A)
Sirdar Big Softie (51% wool, 49% acrylic) super-chunky yarn 1 x 1¾oz (50g) ball (49yd/45m) in shade 319 Graffiti (B)

Needles and equipment
US 10½ (7mm) knitting needles
US 8 (5mm) knitting needles
Yarn sewing needle

Gauge (tension)
11 sts and 16 rows in stockinette (stocking) stitch to a 4-in (10-cm) square on US 10½ (7mm) needles.

Measurements
The finished cowl is 10½in (27cm) across (unstretched) and is 8in (21cm) deep. It should fit an average-sized child from aged 8 to early teens.

Abbreviations
See page 126.

For the cowl
Using US 10½ (7mm) needles, cast on 62 sts in A.
Row 1: [K2, p2] to last 2 sts, k2.
Row 2: [P2, k2] to last 2 sts, p2.
Rep last 2 rows once more.
Work 22 rows in st st beg with a knit row.
Row 27: [K2, p2] to last 2 sts, k2.
Row 28: [P2, k2] to last 2 sts, p2.
Rep rows 27–28 once more.
Bind (cast) off.

Moustache
Left side:
Using US 8 (5mm) knitting needles, cast on 3 sts in B.
Row 1: Inc, k to end. *(4 sts)*
Row 2: Purl.
Rep rows 1–2 once more. *(5 sts)*
Beg with a knit row, work 2 rows in st st.

Row 7: K2tog, k2, m1, k1.
Row 8: Purl.
Rep rows 7–8 once more.
Row 11: K2tog, k to end. *(4 sts)*
Row 12: Purl.
Row 13: K2, ssk. *(3 sts)*
Row 14: Purl.
Row 15: K1, ssk. *(2 sts)*
Row 16: P2tog and fasten off.

Right side:
Using US 8 (5mm) knitting needles, cast on 3 sts in B.
Row 1: K1, inc, k1. *(4 sts)*
Row 2: Purl.
Row 3: K2, inc, k1. *(5 sts)*
Beg with a purl row, work 3 rows in st st.
Row 7: K1, m1, k2, ssk.
Row 8: Purl.
Rep rows 7–8 once more.
Row 11: K3, ssk. *(4 sts)*
Row 12: Purl.
Row 13: K2tog, k2. *(3 sts)*
Row 14: Purl.
Row 15: K2tog, k1. *(2 sts)*
Row 16: P2tog and fasten off.

To make up
Join the back seam using flat stitch (see page 124).
Oversew the two moustache pieces in place, just below the top of the cowl.
Weave in all loose ends.

Techniques

In this section you'll find basic knitting techniques that will let you make most of the scarves in this book. You can substitute the yarn recommended in a pattern with the same weight of yarn in a different brand, but you will need to check the gauge (tension). When calculating the quantity of yarn you require, it is the length of yarn in each ball that you need to check, rather than the weight of the ball; the length of yarn per ball in each recommended project yarn is given in the pattern.

Gauge (tension)

A scarf doesn't need to be a precise size, but a gauge (tension) is given with each pattern to help you make your scarf the same size as the sample. The gauge (tension) is given as the number of stitches and rows you need to work to produce a 4-in (10-cm) square of knitting.

Using the recommended yarn and needles, cast on 8 stitches more than the gauge (tension) instruction asks for—so if you need to have 10 stitches to 4in (10cm), cast on 18 stitches. Working in pattern as instructed, work eight rows more than is needed. Bind (cast) off loosely.

Lay the swatch flat without stretching it. Lay a ruler across the stitches as shown, with the 2in (5cm) mark centered on the knitting, then put a pin in the knitting at the start of the ruler and at the 4in (10cm) mark: the pins should be well away from the edges of the swatch. Count the number of stitches between the pins. Repeat the process across the rows to count the number of rows to 4in (10cm).

If the number of stitches and rows you've counted is the same as the number asked for in the instructions, you have the correct gauge (tension). If you do not have the same number then you will need to change your gauge (tension). To change gauge (tension) you need to change the size of your knitting needles. A good rule of thumb to follow is that one difference in needle size will create a difference of one stitch in the gauge (tension). You will need to use larger needles to achieve fewer stitches and smaller ones to achieve more stitches.

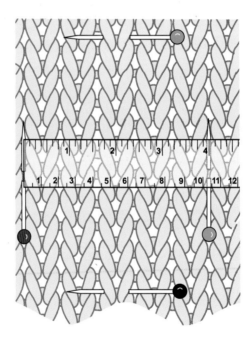

Knitting with two strands at once

A few patterns in this book involve knitting using two strands of the same yarn at once. In most cases, this is quite easy to do by using the main yarn end, then pulling out the beginning of the ball of yarn from the center and knitting them together.

Holding needles

If you are a knitting novice, you will need to discover which is the most comfortable way for you to hold your needles. This applies when using either a pair of knitting needles or a circular needle.

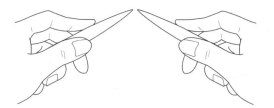 

Like a knife
Pick up the needles, one in each hand, as if you were holding a knife and fork—that is to say, with your hands lightly over the top of each needle. As you knit, you will tuck the blunt end of the right-hand needle under your arm, let go with your hand and use your hand to manipulate the yarn, returning your hand to the needle to move the stitches along.

Like a pen
Now try changing the right hand so you are holding the needle as you would hold a pen, with your thumb and forefinger lightly gripping the needle close to its pointed tip and the shaft resting in the crook of your thumb. As you knit, you will not need to let go of the needle but simply slide your right hand forward to manipulate the yarn.

Holding yarn

As you knit, you will be working stitches off the left needle and on to the right needle, and the yarn you are working with needs to be tensioned and manipulated to produce an even fabric. To hold and tension the yarn you can use either your right or left hand. Try both methods to discover which works best for you.

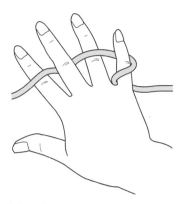 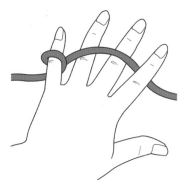

Yarn in right hand
With the ball of yarn on the right, catch the yarn around your little finger then lace it over the third finger, under the middle finger, and over the first finger of your right hand.

Yarn in left hand
With the ball of yarn on your left, catch the yarn around your little finger then take it over the third and middle fingers. Most left-handed knitters will also find that, even if they reverse the direction of knitting (working stitches off the right needle onto the left needle), using the left hand to manipulate the yarn will be easier to manage. To knit and purl in the Continental style (see pages 119 and 120), hold the yarn in your left hand.

Making a slip knot

You will need to make a slip knot to form your first cast-on stitch.

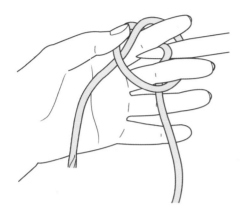

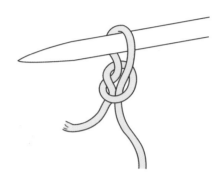

1 With the ball of yarn on your right, lay the end of the yarn on the palm of your left hand and hold it in place with your left thumb. With your right hand, take the yarn around your top two fingers to form a loop. Take the knitting needle through the back of the loop from right to left and use it to pick up the strand nearest to the yarn ball, as shown in the diagram. Pull the strand through to form a loop at the front.

2 Slip the yarn off your fingers leaving the loop on the needle. Gently pull on both yarn ends to tighten the knot. Then pull on the yarn leading to the ball of yarn to tighten the knot on the needle.

Casting on (cable method)

There are a few methods of casting on but the one used for the projects in this book is the cable method, which uses two needles.

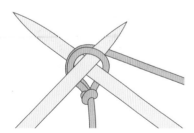

1 Make a slip knot as shown above. Put the needle with the slip knot into your left hand. Insert the point of your other needle into the front of the slip knot and under the left needle. Wind the yarn from the ball of yarn around the tip of the right needle.

2 Using the tip of your needle, draw the yarn through the slip knot to form a loop. This loop is your new stitch. Slip the loop from the right needle onto the left needle.

3 To make the next stitch, insert the tip of your right needle between the two stitches. Wind the yarn over the right needle, from left to right, then draw the yarn through to form a loop. Transfer this loop to your left needle. Repeat until you have cast on the right number of stitches for your project.

Basic stitches

Most people in the English-speaking world knit using a method called English (or American) knitting. However, in parts of Europe, people prefer a method known as Continental knitting. If you are new to knitting, try both techniques to see which works better for you.

Making a knit stitch

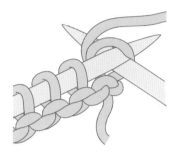

1 Hold the needle with the cast-on stitches in your left hand, and then insert the point of the right needle into the front of the first stitch from left to right. Wind the yarn around the point of the right needle, from left to right.

2 With the tip of your right needle, pull the yarn through the stitch to form a loop. This loop is your new stitch.

3 Slip the original stitch off the left needle by gently pulling your right needle to the right. Repeat these steps till you have knitted all the stitches on your left needle. To work the next row, transfer the needle with all the stitches into your left hand.

Making a knit stitch Continental style

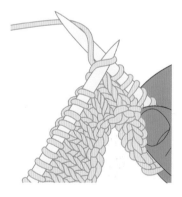
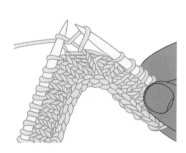
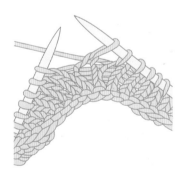

1 Hold the needle with the stitches to be knitted in your left hand, and then insert the tip of the right needle into the front of the first stitch from left to right. Holding the yarn fairly taut with your left hand at the back of your work, use the tip of your right needle to pick up a loop of yarn.

2 With the tip of your right needle, bring the yarn through the original stitch to form a loop. This loop is your new stitch.

3 Slip the original stitch off the left needle by gently pulling your right needle to the right. Repeat these steps till you have knitted all the stitches on your left needle. To work the next row, transfer the needle with all the stitches into your left hand.

Making a purl stitch

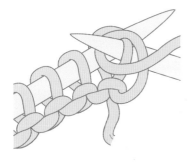  

1 Hold the needle with the stitches in your left hand, and then insert the point of the right needle into the front of the first stitch from right to left. Wind the yarn around the point of the right needle, from right to left.

2 With the tip of the right needle, pull the yarn through the stitch to form a loop. This loop is your new stitch.

3 Slip the original stitch off the left needle by gently pulling your right needle to the right. Repeat these steps till you have purled all the stitches on your left needle. To work the next row, transfer the needle with all the stitches into your left hand.

Making a purl stitch Continental style

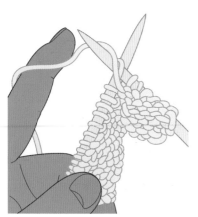 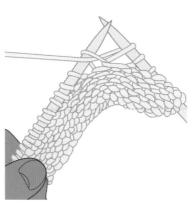 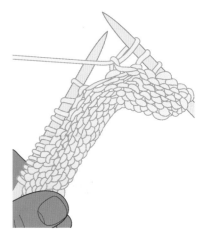

1 Hold the needle with the stitches to be knitted in your left hand, and then insert the tip of the right needle into the front of the first stitch from right to left. Holding the yarn fairly taut at the back of your work, use the tip of your right needle to pick up a loop of yarn.

2 With the tip of your right needle, bring the yarn through the original stitch to form a loop.

3 Slip the original stitch off the left needle by gently pulling your right needle to the right. Repeat these steps till you have purled all the stitches on your left needle. To work the next row, transfer the needle with all the stitches into your left hand.

Binding (casting) off

You need to bind (cast) off your stitches to complete the projects and stop the knitting unraveling.

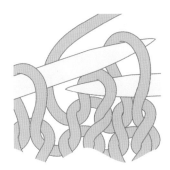

1 First knit two stitches in the normal way. With the point of your left needle, pick up the first stitch you have just knitted and lift it over the second stitch. Knit another stitch so that there are two stitches on your needle again. Repeat the process of lifting the first stitch over the second stitch. Continue this process until there is just one stitch remaining on the right needle.

2 Break the yarn, leaving a tail of yarn long enough to stitch your work together. Pull the tail all the way through the last stitch. Slip the stitch off the needle and pull it fairly tightly to make sure it is secure.

Increasing

There are two methods of increasing used in this book.

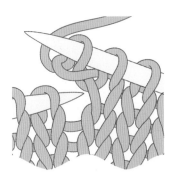

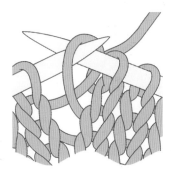

Increase (inc)
Start knitting your stitch in the normal way but instead of slipping the "old" stitch off the needle, knit into the back of it and then slip the "old" stitch off the needle in the normal way. The same principle is used to increase on a purl row, except that you purl the stitches instead of knitting them.

Make one (m1)
Pick up the horizontal strand between two stitches on your left needle. Knit into the back of the loop and transfer the stitch to the right needle in the normal way. (It is important to knit into the back of the loop so that the yarn is twisted and does not form a hole in your work.)

Decreasing

There are three different ways of decreasing used in this book.

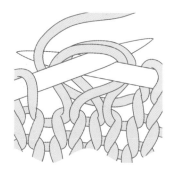

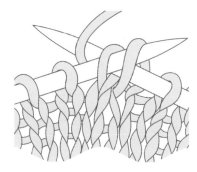

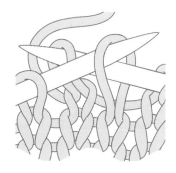

Knit two together (k2tog)
This is the simplest way of decreasing. Simply insert your needle through two stitches instead of the normal one when you begin your stitch and then knit them in the normal way.

The same principle is used to decrease on a purl row, except that you purl the stitches together instead of knitting them.

Slip, slip, knit (ssk)
Slip one stitch knitwise, and then the next stitch knitwise onto your right needle, without knitting them. Then insert the left needle from left to right through the front loops of both the slipped stitches and knit them as normal.

Slip one, knit one, pass the slipped stitch over (skpo)
Slip the first stitch knitwise from the left to the right needle without knitting it. Knit the next stitch. Then lift the slipped stitch over the knitted stitch and drop it off the needle.

Cables

Cables involve moving a group of stitches and are much simpler to work than they look. You will need a cable needle to hold the stitches that are being moved. If the cable is a six-stitch one, then work it as shown here: if it is a four-stitch cable, then slip two stitches onto the needle and knit two, rather than three. For a 12-stitch cable, slip six stitches onto the needle and knit six.

A six-stitch back cable (C6B)

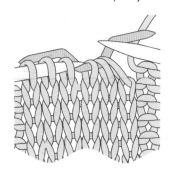

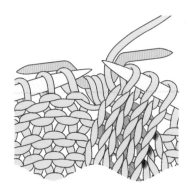

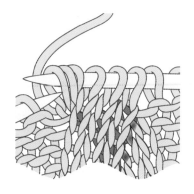

1 Work to the position of the cable. Slip the next three stitches on the left needle onto the cable needle, keeping the cable needle at the back of the work. Leave the three stitches in the middle of the cable needle so they don't slip off.

2 Knit the next three stitches off the left needle in the usual way.

3 Then knit the three stitches off the cable needle and the cable is completed.

A six-stitch front cable (C6F)

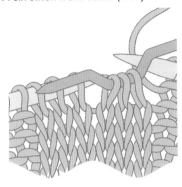 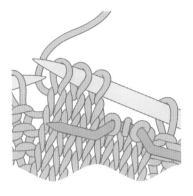 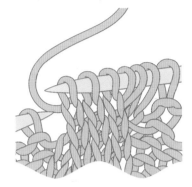

1 Work to the position of the cable. Slip the next three stitches on the left needle onto the cable needle, keeping the cable needle in front of the work. Leave the three stitches on the cable needle in the middle so they don't slip off.

2 Knit the next three stitches off the left needle in the usual way.

3 Then knit the three stitches off the cable needle and the cable is completed.

Picking up stitches

For some projects, you will need to pick up stitches along either a horizontal edge (the cast-on or bound- (cast-) off edge of your knitting), or a vertical edge (the edges of your rows of knitting).

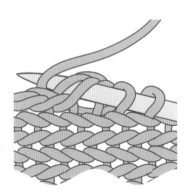 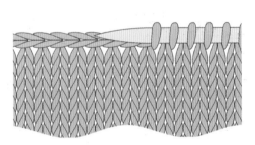

Along a vertical edge

With the right side of the knitting facing you, insert a knitting needle from the front to back between the first and second stitches of the first row. Wind the yarn around the needle and pull through a loop to form the new stitch. Normally you have more gaps between rows than stitches you need to pick up and knit. To make sure your picking up is even, you will have to miss a gap every few rows.

Along a horizontal edge

This is worked in the same way as picking up stitches along a vertical edge, except that you will work through the cast-on or bound- (cast-) off stitches rather than the gaps between rows. You will normally have the same number of stitches to pick up and knit as there are existing stitches.

Mattress stitch

There are two versions of this stitch—one used to join two vertical edges and the other used to join two horizontal edges.

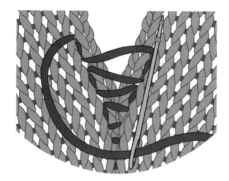

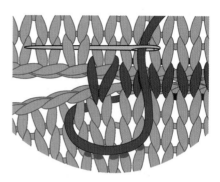

Vertical edges

Place the two edges side by side with the right side facing you. Take a yarn sewing needle under the running thread between the first two stitches of one side, then under the corresponding running thread of the other side. Pull your yarn up fairly firmly every few stitches.

Horizontal edges

Place the two edges side by side with the right side facing you. Take a yarn sewing needle under the two "legs" of the last row of stitches on the first piece of knitting. Then take your needle under the two "legs" of the corresponding stitch on the second piece of knitting. Pull your yarn up fairly firmly every few stitches.

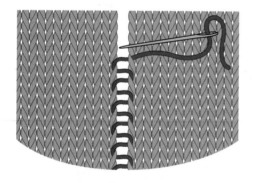

Sewing in ends

The easiest way to finish yarn ends is to run a few small stitches forward then backward through your work, ideally in a seam, or along an edge. It is a good idea to use a yarn sewing needle to do this and take the tail between the strands that make up your yarn, as this will help make sure the tail stays in place.

Flat stitch

Unlike mattress stitch, this stitch creates a join that is completely flat.

Lay the two edges to be joined side by side with the right side facing you. Using a yarn sewing needle, pick up the very outermost strand of knitting from one side and then the other, working your way along the seam and pulling your yarn up firmly every few stitches.

Crochet techniques

While the projects in this book are all knitted rather than crocheted, for the Fur Collar (see page 90) and the Fine Lace-Knit Capelet (see page 97) you will need to know how to work a crochet chain, and for the Patchwork Scarf (see page 77), a crochet edging.

Crochet chain

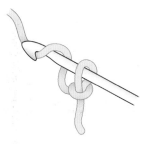

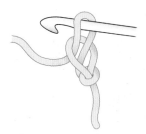

1 Make a slip knot on the crochet hook in the same way as for knitting (see page 118). Holding the slip stitch on the hook, wind the yarn round the hook from the back to the front, then catch the yarn in the crochet-hook tip.

2 Pull the yarn through the slip stitch on the crochet hook to make the second link in the chain. Continue in this way till the chain is the length that you need.

Crochet edging

A crochet edging can be worked along a horizontal edge or a vertical edge, but the basic technique is the same.

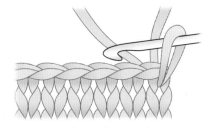

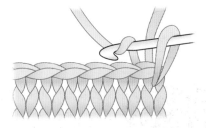

1 Insert the crochet hook in the first space between stitches. Wind the yarn round the hook and pull a loop of yarn through.

2 Wind the yarn round the hook again and then pull the loop through to make a single chain.

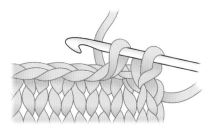

3 Insert the hook through the next stitch, wind the yarn round the hook, and pull through a second loop of yarn.

4 Wind the yarn round the hook and pull a loop of yarn through both loops on the hook. Repeat steps 3 and 4, inserting the hook into the spaces between stitches in an even pattern.

For crochet edging along a vertical edge, insert your hook into the spaces between the edges of the rows rather than the spaces between stitches.

Abbreviations

beg	begin(ning)
C6B	cable six back: see page 122
C6(12)F	cable six (twelve) front: see pages 122-123
cm	centimeter(s)
cont	continue
g	gram(s)
in	inch(es)
inc	increase, by working into front and back of next stitch: see page 121
k	knit
k2tog	knit two stitches together, to decrease: see page 122
m1	make one stitch, by knitting into the strand between two stitches, to increase: see page 121
m	meter(s)
mm	millimeter
oz	ounces
p	purl
patt	pattern
p2tog	purl two stitches together, to decrease: see page 122
psso	pass slipped stitch over, pass a slipped stitch over another stitch
pwise	purlwise, slip a stitch as if you were going to purl it
rem	remain(ing)
rep	repeat
RS	right side
skpo	slip one stitch, knit one stitch, pass slipped stitch over knitted one, to decrease: see page 122
sl1	slip one stitch, from the left-hand needle to the right-hand needle without knitting it
ssk	slip one stitch, slip one stitch, knit slipped stitches together, to decrease: see page 122
st(s)	stitch(es)
st st	stockinette (stocking) stitch
tbl	through the back loop, knit or purl though the back of the stitch
WS	wrong side
yb	yarn back, between the tips of the needles
yd	yard(s)
yf	yarn forward, between the tips of the needles
yo	yarn over, wrap yarn around needle between stitches, to increase and to make an eyelet
yo2	wrap yarn twice around needle between stitches, to make a large eyelet
[ ]	work instructions within square brackets as directed
*	work instructions after/between asterisk(s) as directed

Author's acknowledgments

My thanks to Cindy Richards, Penny Craig, Fahema Khanam, and everyone at CICO Books. Thanks also to Kate Haxell, my editor, Marilyn Wilson, the pattern checker, Terry Benson, the photographer, and Luis Peral, the stylist. I should also like to thank my sister, Louise Turner, for her help with the knitting, and my ever-patient partner, Roger Dromard, and son, Louis.

I would like to thank Rowan for supplying much of the yarn used in this book.
www.knitrowan.com

Publisher's acknowledgments

The publishers would like to thank the following companies for lending goods for photography:

Oliver Bonas
147–148 Upper Street
London N1 1RA
www.oliverbonas.com

Present And Correct
23 Arlington Way
London EC1R 1UY
www.presentandcorrect.com

Preloved by Melina
36 Amhurst Road
London E8 1JN
Tel: 07591 541564
Email: bpreloved@ymail.com

INDEX

SUPPLIERS

USA

Knitting Fever Inc.
PO Box 336
315 Bayview Avenue
Amityville
NY 11701
Tel: +1 516 546 3600
www.knittingfever.com
Debbie Bliss, Katia, Noro, Sirdar,
Sublime

Lion Brand Yarns
Tel: +800 258 YARN (9276)
Online sales and store locator on
website
www.lionbrand.com

Westminster Fibers
165 Ledge Street
Nashua
NH 03060
Tel: +800 445 9276
www.westminsterfibers.com
Rowan

Canada

Diamond Yarn
155 Martin Ross Avenue, Unit 3
Toronto, ON
M3J 2L9
Tel: +1 416 736 6111
www.diamondyarn.com
Debbie Bliss, Katia, Noro, Sirdar,
Sublime

Westminster Fibers
10 Roybridge Gate, Suite 200
Vaughn, ON
L4H 3MB
Tel: +800 263 2354
www.westminsterfibers.com
Rowan

UK

Debbie Bliss Yarns
Designer Yarns Ltd
Units 8–10 Newbridge Industrial Estate
Pitt Street, Keighley
West Yorkshire BD21 4PQ
Tel: +44 (0) 1535 664222
www.debbieblissonline.com

Katia Yarns
Barcelona, Spain
Tel: +34 93 828 38 19
www.katia.com
Website gives details of local
UK suppliers

Rowan
Rowan Yarns
Green Lane Mill
Holmfirth
West Yorkshire HD9 2DX
Tel: +44 (0) 1484 681881
www.knitrowan.com

Sirdar
Sirdar Spinning Ltd
Flanshaw Lane
Wakefield
West Yorkshire WF2 9ND
Tel: +44 (0) 1924 231682
www.sirdar.co.uk

Deramores
Online store only
Tel: 0800 488 0708
www.deramores.com
Jenny Watson, Lion Brand, Noro,
Sublime, and others

John Lewis
Retail stores and online
www.johnlewis.com
Telephone numbers of local stores on
website
Tel: 08456 049049

Mavis Crafts
Online and retail store
Tel: +44 (0) 208 950 5445
www.mavis-crafts.com
Katia, Sirdar, Sublime

Australia

Prestige Yarns Pty Ltd
PO Box 39
Bulli
NSW 2516
Tel: +61 (0)2 4285 6669
www.prestigeyarns.com.au
Debbie Bliss

Texyarns International PTY Ltd
PO Box 599
South Yarra
VIC 3141
Tel: +61 (0)3 9427 9009
www.texyarns.com
Katia

Rowan
www.knitrowan.com
Online store locator

Black Sheep Wool 'n' Wares
Tel +61 (0)2 6779 1196
www.blacksheepwool.com.au
Debbie Bliss, Katia, Noro, Sirdar,
Sublime

Creative Images Crafts
PO Box 106
Hastings
VIC 3915
Tel: +61 (0)3 5979 1555
Sirdar